Praise for Valentine Delights
A Collection of Valentine Recipes
Cookbook Delights Holiday Series - Book 2

…"Each year I like to search for fun, new, and creative ways to surprise my sweetheart on Valentines Day. Since discovering **Valentine Delights Cookbook**, I've been able to come up with some of the most thoughtful and inventive ways to celebrate!

I've drawn romantic ideas from the hundreds of recipes on these pages, including two of our favorites – *Caviar Heart Kisses* and *Heart-Shaped Pizza*. The poetry and "The Language of Flowers" also add ambiance to the occasion.

There are many ideas in this cookbook to help you show your children and friends just how much they mean to you as well. Treat yourself or someone you love to a copy of this cookbook today!"…

Kimberly Carter
Publicist

…"**Valentine Delights Cookbook** with its romantic poetry, folklore, history, and other wonderful informational sections, as well as festive and delicious recipes, is a must-have holiday book for any valentine lover.

Before buying any flowers, consult **Valentine Delights** "Colors and Symbolism of Flowers" section to find just the right flower to say the message you want to convey. This book has it all!

Valentine Delights Cookbook will soon be part of your treasured collection of splendid holiday books to be passed down to future generations."…

Mary Scripture-Smith
Graphic Designer

Praise for Valentine Delights
A Collection of Valentine Recipes
Cookbook Delights Holiday Series - Book 2

…"Whispering Pine Press International has done it again with the newest in their Holiday Cookbook Delights Series collection. *Valentine Delights Cookbook* continues the legacy of high quality work and craftsmanship from its author. The recipes are all neatly organized and easy to follow. Detailed indices make it easy to find favorite recipes. The recipes seem very versatile, as well. They can be modified to fit a romantic Valentine's dinner for two, or to fit a feast of family and friends. Although the book is specific to one holiday all of the dishes can be prepared and served year round. This cookbook is great to have at your fingertips all year round."…

Allyson Schnabel
Editor, Teacher

…"*Valentine Delights Cookbook* is not only a cookbook, but a wealth of information about Valentine's Day. It includes fascinating facts, folklore, history of Valentine's Day, Valentine symbols, Valentine's Day Language of Flowers, and poetry. It even includes information on Valentine types.

In addition to all this information it has a collection of over 260 recipes that are delicious, and will be enjoyed by your family and friends.

This is a great value for the price and makes a wonderful gift."…

Dr. James G. Hood
Editor

ii

Praise for Valentine Delights
A Collection of Valentine Recipes
Cookbook Delights Holiday Series - Book 2

... "With the world as it is today it's easy to be distracted. We often put the ones we love most on the back burner. That's why Valentine's Day is so important. It gives us the chance to truly show how much we love that someone special.

Valentine Delights Cookbook brings your romance to a full boil! What better way to say "I love you" than to make something with your hand from your heart? Or better yet, make one of the hundreds of recipes together. You will bind as you play together making these mouthwatering treats. If you prefer, you can plan the entire evening with the help of this cookbook.

Valentine Delights Cookbook not only has recipes, but it includes a full guide that explains the meaning behind a large array of plants and flowers. With this you can build a luscious bouquet that has its own unique story.

Sit down and enjoy this book. Share the poetry. Savor its delights, and cherish each other."...

Ed Archambeault
Spokane, WA.

Valentine Delights

A Collection of Valentine Recipes

Cookbook Delights Holiday Series - Book 2

Karen Jean Matsko Hood

Current and Future Cookbooks
By Karen Jean Matsko Hood

DELIGHTS SERIES

Almond Delights
Anchovy Delights
Apple Delights
Apricot Delights
Artichoke Delights
Asparagus Delights
Avocado Delights
Banana Delights
Barley Delights
Basil Delights
Bean Delights
Beef Delights
Beer Delights
Beet Delights
Blackberry Delights
Blueberry Delights
Bok Choy Delights
Boysenberry Delights
Brazil Nut Delights
Broccoli Delights
Brussels Sprouts Delights
Buffalo Berry Delights
Butter Delights
Buttermilk Delights
Cabbage Delights
Calamari Delights
Cantaloupe Delights
Caper Delights
Cardamom Delights
Carrot Delights
Cashew Delights
Cauliflower Delights
Celery Delights
Cheese Delights
Cherry Delights
Chestnut Delights
Chicken Delights
Chili Pepper Delights
Chive Delights
Chocolate Delights
Chokecherry Delights
Cilantro Delights
Cinnamon Delights
Clam Delights
Clementine Delights
Coconut Delights
Coffee Delights
Conch Delights
Corn Delights
Cottage Cheese Delights
Crab Delights
Cranberry Delights
Cucumber Delights
Cumin Delights
Curry Delights
Date Delights
Edamame Delights
Egg Delights
Eggplant Delights
Elderberry Delights
Endive Delights
Fennel Delights
Fig Delights
Filbert (Hazelnut) Delights
Fish Delights
Garlic Delights
Ginger Delights
Ginseng Delights
Goji Berry Delights
Grape Delights
Grapefruit Delights
Grapple Delights
Guava Delights
Ham Delights
Hamburger Delights
Herb Delights
Herbal Tea Delights
Honey Delights
Honeyberry Delights
Honeydew Delights
Horseradish Delights

Huckleberry Delights
Jalapeño Delights
Jerusalem Artichoke Delights
Jicama Delights
Kale Delights
Kiwi Delights
Kohlrabi Delights
Lavender Delights
Leek Delights
Lemon Delights
Lentil Delights
Lettuce Delights
Lime Delights
Lingonberry Delights
Lobster Delights
Loganberry Delights
Macadamia Nut Delights
Mango Delights
Marionberry Delights
Milk Delights
Mint Delights
Miso Delights
Mushroom Delights
Mussel Delights
Nectarine Delights
Oatmeal Delights
Olive Delights
Onion Delights
Orange Delights
Oregon Berry Delights
Oyster Delights
Papaya Delights
Parsley Delights
Parsnip Delights
Pea Delights
Peach Delights
Peanut Delights
Pear Delights
Pecan Delights
Pepper Delights
Persimmon Delights
Pine Nut Delights
Pineapple Delights
Pistachio Delights
Plum Delights

Pomegranate Delights
Pomelo Delights
Popcorn Delights
Poppy Seed Delights
Pork Delights
Potato Delights
Prickly Pear Cactus Delights
Prune Delights
Pumpkin Delights
Quince Delights
Quinoa Delights
Radish Delights
Raisin Delights
Raspberry Delights
Rhubarb Delights
Rice Delights
Rose Delights
Rosemary Delights
Rutabaga Delights
Salmon Delights
Salmonberry Delights
Salsify Delights
Savory Delights
Scallop Delights
Seaweed Delights
Serviceberry Delights
Sesame Delights
Shallot Delights
Shrimp Delights
Soybean Delights
Spinach Delights
Squash Delights
Star Fruit Delights
Strawberry Delights
Sunflower Seed Delights
Sweet Potato Delights
Swiss Chard Delights
Tangerine Delights
Tapioca Delights
Tayberry Delights
Tea Delights
Teaberry Delights
Thimbleberry Delights
Tofu Delights
Tomatillo Delights

Tomato Delights
Trout Delights
Truffle Delights
Tuna Delights
Turkey Delights
Turmeric Delights
Turnip Delights
Vanilla Delights
Walnut Delights
Wasabi Delights
Watermelon Delights
Wheat Delights
Wild Rice Delights
Yam Delights
Yogurt Delights
Zucchini Delights

CITY DELIGHTS
Chicago Delights
Coeur d'Alene Delights
Great Falls Delights
Honolulu Delights
Minneapolis Delights
Phoenix Delights
Portland Delights
Sandpoint Delights
Scottsdale Delights
Seattle Delights
Spokane Delights
St. Cloud Delights

FOSTER CARE
Foster Children Cookbook
  and Activity Book
Foster Children's Favorite
  Recipes
Holiday Cookbook for
  Foster Families

GENERAL THEME
  DELIGHTS
Appetizer Delights
Baby Food Delights
Barbeque Delights
Beer-Making Delights
Beverage Delights

Biscotti Delights
Bisque Delights
Blender Delights
Bread Delights
Bread Maker Delights
Breakfast Delights
Brunch Delights
Cake Delights
Campfire Food Delights
Candy Delights
Canned Food Delights
Cast Iron Delights
Cheesecake Delights
Chili Delights
Chowder Delights
Cocktail Delights
College Cooking Delights
Comfort Food Delights
Cookie Delights
Cooking for One Delights
Cooking for Two Delights
Cracker Delights
Crepe Delights
Crockpot Delights
Dairy Delights
Dehydrated Food Delights
Dessert Delights
Dinner Delights
Dutch Oven Delights
Foil Delights
Fondue Delights
Food Processor Delights
Fried Food Delights
Frozen Food Delights
Fruit Delights
Gelatin Delights
Grilled Delights
Hiking Food Delights
Ice Cream Delights
Juice Delights
Kid's Delights
Kosher Diet Delights
Liqueur-Making Delights
Liqueurs and Spirits Delights
Lunch Delights

Marinade Delights
Microwave Delights
Milk Shake and Malt Delights
Panini Delights
Pasta Delights
Pesto Delights
Phyllo Delights
Pickled Food Delights
Picnic Food Delights
Pizza Delights
Preserved Delights
Pudding and Custard Delights
Quiche Delights
Quick Mix Delights
Rainbow Delights
Salad Delights
Salsa Delights
Sandwich Delights
Sea Vegetable Delights
Seafood Delights
Smoothie Delights
Snack Delights
Soup Delights
Supper Delights
Tart Delights
Torte Delights
Tropical Delights
Vegan Delights
Vegetable Delights
Vegetarian Delights
Vinegar Delights
Wildflower Delights
Wine Delights
Winemaking Delights
Wok Delights

GIFTS-IN-A-JAR SERIES
Beverage Gifts-in-a-Jar
Christmas Gifts-in-a-Jar
Cookie Gifts-in-a-Jar
Gifts-in-a-Jar
Gifts-in-a-Jar Catholic
Gifts-in-a-Jar Christian
Holiday Gifts-in-a-Jar
Soup Gifts-in-a-Jar

HEALTH-RELATED DELIGHTS
Achalasia Diet Delights
Adrenal Health Diet Delights
Anti-Acid Reflux Diet Delights
Anti-Cancer Diet Delights
Anti-Inflammation Diet
  Delights
Anti-Stress Diet Delights
Arthritis Delights
Bone Health Diet Delights
Diabetic Diet Delights
Diet for Pink Delights
Fibromyalgia Diet Delights
Gluten-Free Diet Delights
Healthy Breath Diet Delights
Healthy Digestion Diet
  Delights
Healthy Heart Diet Delights
Healthy Skin Diet Delights
Healthy Teeth Diet Delights
High-Fiber Diet Delights
High-Iodine Diet Delights
High-Protein Diet Delights
Immune Health Diet Delights
Kidney Health Diet Delights
Lactose-Free Diet Delights
Liquid Diet Delights
Liver Health Diet Delights
Low-Calorie Diet Delights
Low-Carb Diet Delights
Low-Fat Diet Delights
Low-Sodium Diet Delights
Low-Sugar Diet Delights
Lymphoma Health Support
  Diet Delights
Multiple Sclerosis Healthy
  Diet Delights
No Flour No Sugar Diet
  Delights
Organic Food Delights
pH-Friendly Diet Delights
Pregnancy Diet Delights
Raw Food Diet Delights
Sjögren's Syndrome Diet
  Delights
Soft Food Diet Delights
Thyroid Health Diet Delights

Fijian Delights
French Delights
German Delights
Greek Delights
Hungarian Delights
Icelandic Delights
Indian Delights
Irish Delights
Italian Delights
Korean Delights
Mexican Delights
Native American Delights
Polish Delights
Russian Delights
Scottish Delights
Slovenian Delights
Swedish Delights
Thai Delights
The Netherlands Delights
Yugoslavian Delights
Zambian Delights

REGIONAL DELIGHTS
Glacier National Park Delights
Northwest Regional Delights
Oregon Coast Delights
Schweitzer Mountain Delights
Southwest Regional Delights
Tropical Delights
Washington Wine Country
  Delights
Wine Delights of Walla
  Walla Wineries
Yellowstone National Park
  Delights

SEASONAL DELIGHTS
Autumn Harvest Delights
Spring Harvest Delights
Summer Harvest Delights
Winter Harvest Delights

SPECIAL EVENTS
   DELIGHTS
Birthday Delights

Coffee Klatch Delights
Super Bowl Delights
Tea Time Delights

STATE DELIGHTS
Alaska Delights
Arizona Delights
Georgia Delights
Hawaii Delights
Idaho Delights
Illinois Delights
Iowa Delights
Louisiana Delights
Minnesota Delights
Montana Delights
North Dakota Delights
Oregon Delights
South Dakota Delights
Texas Delights
Washington Delights

U.S. TERRITORIES
   DELIGHTS
Cruzan Delights
U.S. Virgin Island Delights

MISCELLANEOUS
   COOKBOOKS
Getaway Studio Cookbook
The Soup Doctor's Cookbook

BILINGUAL DELIGHTS
   SERIES
Apple Delights, English-
  French Edition
Apple Delights, English-
  Russian Edition
Apple Delights, English-
  Spanish Edition
Huckleberry Delights,
  English-French Edition
Huckleberry Delights,
  English-Russian Edition
Huckleberry Delights,
  English-Spanish Edition

CATHOLIC DELIGHTS SERIES
Apple Delights Catholic
Coffee Delights Catholic
Easter Delights Catholic
Huckleberry Delights Catholic
Tea Delights Catholic

CATHOLIC BILINGUAL DELIGHTS SERIES
Apple Delights Catholic, English-French Edition
Apple Delights Catholic, English-Russian Edition
Apple Delights Catholic, English-Spanish Edition
Huckleberry Delights Catholic, English-Spanish Edition

CHRISTIAN DELIGHTS SERIES
Apple Delights Christian
Coffee Delights Christian
Easter Delights Christian
Huckleberry Delights Christian
Tea Delights Christian

CHRISTIAN BILINGUAL DELIGHTS SERIES
Apple Delights Christian, English-French Edition
Apple Delights Christian, English-Russian Edition
Apple Delights Christian, English-Spanish Edition
Huckleberry Delights Christian, English-Spanish Edition

FUNDRAISING COOKBOOKS
Ask about our fundraising cookbooks to help raise funds for your organization.

The above books are also available in bilingual versions. Please contact Whispering Pine Press International, Inc., for details.

Please note that some books are future books and are currently in production. Please contact us for availability date. Prices are subject to change without notice.

The above list of books is not all-inclusive. For a complete list please visit our website or contact us at:

Whispering Pine Press International, Inc.
Your Northwest Book Publishing Company
P.O. Box 214
Spokane Valley, WA 99037-0214 USA
Phone: (509) 928-8700 | Fax: (509) 922-9949
Email: sales@whisperingpinepress.com
Publisher Websites: www.WhisperingPinePress.com
www.WhisperingPinePressBookstore.com
Blog: www.WhisperingPinePressBlog.com

Valentine Delights

A Collection of Valentine Recipes
Cookbook Delights Holiday Series - Book 2

Karen Jean Matsko Hood

Published by:

Whispering Pine Press International, Inc.

Your Northwest Book Publishing Company
P.O. Box 214
Spokane Valley, WA 99037-0214 USA
Phone: (509) 928-8700 | Fax: (509) 922-9949
Email: sales@whisperingpinepress.com
Publisher Websites: www.WhisperingPinePress.com
www.WhisperingPinePressBookstore.com
Blog: www.WhisperingPinePressBlog.com
SAN 253-200X
Printed in the U.S.A.

Published by Whispering Pine Press International, Inc.
P.O. Box 214
Spokane Valley, Washington 99037-0214 USA

For sales outside the United States, please contact the Whispering Pine Press International, Inc., International Sales Department.

Manufactured in the United States of America. This paper is acid-free and 100% chlorine free.

Book and Cover Design by Artistic Design Service
P.O. Box 1792
Spokane Valley, WA 99037-1792 USA
www.ArtisticDesignService.com

Library of Congress Number LCCN: 2014900295

Hood, Karen Jean Matsko
    Title: Valentine Delights Cookbook: A Collection of Valentine Recipes: Cookbook Delights Holiday Series - Book 2

    p.   cm.

ISBN: 978-1-59649-297-4   case bound
ISBN: 978-1-59649-292-9   perfect bound
ISBN: 978-1-59649-294-3   spiral bound
ISBN: 978-1-59649-293-6   comb bound
ISBN: 978-1-59649-295-0   E-PDF
ISBN: 978-1-59210-349-2   E-PUB
ISBN: 978-1-59434-871-6   E-PRC

First Edition: January 2014
1. Cookery *(Valentine Delights Cookbook: A Collection of Valentine Recipes: Cookbook Delights Holiday Series - Book 2)*   1. Title

Valentine Delights Cookbook
A Collection of Valentine Recipes
Cookbook Delights Holiday Series - Book 2

Gift Inscription

To:_____

From: _____

Date: _____

Special Message: _____

_____

_____

_____

_____

_____

_____

_____

It is always nice to receive a personal note to create a special memory.

www.ValentineDelights.com
www.WhisperingPinePress.com
www.WhisperingPinePressBookstore.com

Dedications

To my husband and best friend, Jim.

To our seventeen children: Gabriel, Brianne Kristina and her husband Moulik Vinodkumar Kothari, Marissa Kimberly and her husband Kevin Matthew Franck, Janelle Karina and her husband Paul Joseph Turcotte, Mikayla Karlene, Kyler James, Kelsey Katrina, Corbin Joel, Caleb Jerome, Keisha Kalani Hiwot, Devontay Joshua, Kianna Karielle Selam, Rosy Kiara, Mercedes Katherine, Jasmine Khalia Wengel, Cheyenne Krystal, and Annalise Kaylee Marie.

To our grandchildren and foster grandchildren: Courtney, Lorenzo, and Leah.

To my brother, Stephen, and his wife, Karen.

To my husband's ten siblings: Gary, Colleen, John, Dan, Mary, Ray, Ann, Teresa, Barbara, Agnes, and their families.

In loving memory of my mom, who passed away in 2007; my dad, who passed away in 1976; and my sister, Sandy, who passed away due to multiple sclerosis in 1999.

To Sandy's three sons: Monte, Bradley, and Derek. To Monte's wife, Sarah, and their children: Liam, Alice, Charlie, and Samuel. To Bradley's wife, Shawnda, and their children: Anton, Isaac, and Isabel.

To our foster children past and present: Krystal, Sara, Rebecca, Janice, Devontay Joshua, Mercedes Katherine, Zha'Nell, Makia, Onna, Cheyenne Krystal, Onna Marie, Nevaeh, and Zada, our future foster children, and all foster children everywhere.

To the Court Appointed Special Advocate (CASA) Volunteer Program in the judicial system which benefits abused and neglected children.

To the Literacy Campaign dedicated to promoting literacy throughout the world.

Acknowledgements

The author would like to acknowledge all those individuals who helped me during my time in writing this book. Appreciation is extended for all their support and effort they put into this project.

Deep gratitude and profound thanks are owed to my husband, Jim, for giving freely of his time and encouragement during this project. Also, thanks are owed to my children Gabriel, Brianne Kristina and her husband Moulik Vinodkumar Kothari, Marissa Kimberly and her husband Kevin Matthew Franck, Janelle Karina and her husband Paul Joseph Turcotte, Mikayla Karlene, Kyler James, Kelsey Katrina, Corbin Joel, Caleb Jerome, Keisha Kalani Hiwot, Devontay Joshua, Kianna Karielle Selam, Rosy Kiara, Mercedes Katherine, Jasmine Khalia Wengel, Cheyenne Krystal, and Annalise Kaylee Marie. All of these persons inspire my writing.

Thanks are due to Sharron Thompson for her assistance in editing and typing this manuscript for publication. Thanks go to Artistic Design Service for their assistance in formatting and providing a graphic design of this manuscript for publication. This project could not have been completed without them.

Many thanks are due to members of my family, all of whom were very supportive during the time it took to complete this project. Their patience and support are greatly appreciated.

Valentine Delights Cookbook
Table of Contents

Valentine Delights Cookbook
A Collection of Valentine Recipes
Cookbook Delights Holiday Series - Book 2

Introduction

Valentine's Day is both a romantic and special family holiday, making it a perfect occasion upon which to design a cookbook!

The recipes in this book have been collected around the themes, colors, and symbols of Valentine's Day. These recipes are great for Valentine's Day, but can also be used every day. We hope you enjoy reading it as well as trying out all the recipes.

This cookbook is designed for easy use and is organized into convenient alphabetical sections: appetizers and dips; beverages; breads and rolls; breakfasts; cakes; candies; cookies; desserts; dressings, sauces, and condiments; jams, jellies, and syrups; main dishes; pies; preserving; salads; side dishes; soups; and wine and spirits.

As a poet, I found it enjoyable to color this cookbook with poetry so that readers could savor the metaphorical richness of Valentine's Day as well as the literal flavors of the valentine recipes. Do enjoy your reading about Valentine's Day, but most importantly, have fun with those you care about while you are cooking.

Be sure to look at the list of current and future cookbooks for other titles in the *Cookbook Delights Series* of books that you might desire. If you do not find the subject you are looking for, please email us with your suggestion for consideration in our list of current and future cookbooks. You may email us at sales@whisperingpinepress.com.

Following is a collection of recipes gathered and modified to bring you *Valentine Delights Cookbook: A Collection of Valentine Recipes, Cookbook Delights Holiday Series - Book 2* by Karen Jean Matsko Hood.

20

Valentine Delights Cookbook
A Collection of Valentine Recipes
Cookbook Delights Holiday Series - Book 2

Valentine's Day Facts

Valentine's Day Facts

St. Valentine's Day falls on February 14th, and it is the traditional day on which lovers in certain cultures let each other know about their love, commonly by sending Valentine's cards, which are often anonymous. The day's associations with romantic love arrived after the High Middle Ages, during which the concept of courtly romantic love was formulated.

The day is now most closely associated with the mutual exchange of love notes in the form of "Valentines." Modern Valentine symbols include the heart-shaped outline and the figure of the winged Cupid. Since the nineteenth century, the practice of handwriting notes has largely given way to the exchange of mass-produced greeting cards. The Greeting Card Association estimates that, world-wide, approximately one billion Valentine cards are sent each year, making the day the second largest card-sending holiday of the year behind Christmas. The association also estimates that women purchase approximately 85 percent of all Valentines.

The first greeting card was a Valentine given in the fifteenth century. It is on display in the British Museum in London.

Along with greeting cards, more than 50 million roses are given for Valentine's Day each year.

Candy is also a favorite gift of the holiday. This tradition of giving candy for Valentine's Day did not become popular until the nineteenth century.

Valentine Delights Cookbook
A Collection of Valentine Recipes
Cookbook Delights Holiday Series - Book 2

Valentine's Day Folklore

Valentine's Day Folklore

During the fifteenth century in England and France the idea of celebrating Valentine's Day first became popular. No one is exactly sure why February was chosen as the date for this holiday, but there are a few explanations.

February 14th was traditionally the day on which birds paired off to mate, hence the association of St. Valentine's Day with romantic love. By the seventeenth century, a valentine was extended to be a gift given, usually some pretty token. It was common during that era for lovers to exchange notes on this day and to call each other their "Valentine." It is probable that many of the legends about St. Valentine were invented during this period, among them being assertions that on the evening before St. Valentine was to be martyred for being a Christian, he passed a love note to his jailer's daughter which read, "From your Valentine."

During a ban on marriages of Roman soldiers by the Emperor Claudius II, St. Valentine secretly helped arrange marriages of soldiers. In most versions of these legends, February 14th is the date associated with his martyrdom.

In ancient Rome, at the festival of Lupercus, the god of fertility was represented as half-naked and dressed in goat skins. As part of the purification ritual, the priests of Lupercus would sacrifice goats to the god, and after drinking wine, they would run through the streets of Rome holding pieces of the goat skin above their heads, touching anyone they met. Young women especially would come forth voluntarily for the occasion, in the belief that being so touched would render them fruitful and bring easy childbirth.

Valentine Delights Cookbook
A Collection of Valentine Recipes
Cookbook Delights Holiday Series - Book 2

Valentine's Day History

Valentine's Day History

The history of Valentine's Day can be traced back to an obscure Catholic Church feast day, said to be in honor of St. Valentine. The connection between St. Valentine and romantic love is not mentioned in any early histories and is regarded by secular historians as purely a matter of legend.

The feast of St. Valentine was first declared to be on February 14th by Pope Gelasius I in 496. There is a widespread legend that he created the day to counter the practice held on Lupercalia of young men and women pairing off as lovers by drawing their names out of an urn, but this practice is not attested in any sources from that era.

Valentine's Day was probably imported into North America in the nineteenth century with settlers from Britain. In the United States, the first mass-produced Valentines of embossed paper lace were produced and sold shortly after 1847 by Esther Howland (1828 – 1904) of Worcester, Massachusetts. Her father operated a large book and stationery store, and she took her inspiration from an English Valentine she had received. In the United States in the second half of the twentieth century, the practice of exchanging cards was extended to include the giving of all manner of gifts, usually from a man to a woman. Such gifts typically include roses and chocolates. Starting in the 1980s, the diamond industry began to promote Valentine's Day as an occasion for giving fine jewelry.

Valentine Delights Cookbook
A Collection of Valentine Recipes
Cookbook Delights Holiday Series - Book 2

The Language of Flowers

The Language of Flowers

The language of flowers, sometimes called floriography, was a Victorian-era means of communication in which various flowers and floral arrangements were used to send coded messages, allowing individuals to express feelings which otherwise could not be spoken. King Charles II brought the art to Sweden from Persia in the seventeenth century. The nuances of the language are now mostly forgotten, but red roses still suggest virtue and chastity; and yellow roses still stand for friendship or devotion—these may not be the exact translations of the Victorian sentiments, but flowers still speak to us.

Others with commonly known meanings are sunflowers, which can mean either haughtiness or respect – they were the favorite flower of St. Julie Billiart for this reason. The iris, being named for the messenger of the gods in Greek mythology, still represents a message being sent. A pansy represents thoughts, a daffodil, fame, and a string of ivy signifies fidelity.

We have compiled a list of flowers and their meanings, and though none of what we have given you has been verified, we have been informed that this is the most current information. Do enjoy your reading on the subject of flowers and their meanings.

Colors and Symbolism of Flowers and Herbs
(In Alphabetical order)

It is interesting to know the symbolism behind the flowers you select for Valentine messages.

Acacia
elegance, friendship, secret love, chaste love, beauty in retirement

Allspice
compassion

Almond
hope, lovers' charm

Aloe
grief

Amaranth
fidelity

Amaryllis
splendid beauty; pride, timidity

Ambrosia
returned love

Amethyst
admiration, undying love

Anemone
truth, unfading love, sincerity, anticipation, forsaken, fading hope

Angelica
inspiration

Aniseed
restoration of youth

Apple (Blossom)
preference, good fortune

Arum
ardor

Azalea
temperance, fragile passion, Chinese symbol of womanhood, take care of yourself

Baby's Breath
everlasting love, pure in heart, happiness

Bells of Ireland
good luck

Basil (Sweet)
best wishes, love, hatred

Bachelor's Buttons
single blessedness, hope in love, celibacy

Bluebell
humility, constancy

Buttercup
childishness, ingratitude

Broom
humility, neatness

Cactus
warmth, endurance, grandeur

Calla
magnificent beauty

Camellia
you're adorable, longing, a flame in my heart

Cedar
I live for thee, think of me

Chamomile
patience, attracts wealth

Chickweed
meet me, rendezvous

Chrysanthemum, red
love you

Chrysanthemum, white
truth

Chrysanthemum, yellow
slighted

Clover Four Leaved
good luck, be mine
Coriander
lust
Cowslip
pensiveness, winning grace
Crocus
cheerfulness, abuse not, joy
Daisy
innocence, purity, faith,
simplicity
Daffodil
regards, deceit, unrequited love
Dandelion
wishes come true, faithfulness,
rustic oracle
Dogwood
durability
Elm
dignity
Eucalyptus
protection
Fennel
worthy of all praise, strength
Fern
sincerity, confidence and
shelter
Forget Me Not
don't forget me, true love,
memories
Garlic
courage, strength
Geranium
friendship, preference
Gladiolus
love at first sight, strength of
character
Grass
submission, utility
Hazelnut
reconciliation

Heliotrope
devotion, eternal love,
faithfulness
Hibiscus
delicate beauty
Hollyhock
female ambition
Honesty
honesty, fascination
Honeysuckle
generous and devoted
affection, sweetness of
disposition
Iris
faith, hope, wisdom and valor,
eloquence, message
Ivy
fidelity, friendship, affection,
marriage
Jasmine
cheerful, wealth, gracefulness
Jonquil
desire, return my affection,
sympathy
Juniper
protection
Lavender
devotion, distrust
Laurel
glory, ambition
Lemon
zest, brings love
Lilac
first love
Lily
heavenly, purity of heart
Lime Tree
conjugal love
Liverwort
confidence
Lobelia

malevolence
Lily of the Valley
return to happiness
Marigold
comfort the heart, grief,
jealousy
Marjoram
blushes, joy and happiness
Mimosa
sensitivity
Mistletoe
kiss me, I surmount difficulties
Myrtle
love, love in absence,
remembrance
Narcissus
formality, stay sweet
Olive
peace
Oleander
caution, beware
Orchid
love, beauty, flattery
Pansy
thoughts for you, love
Peach Blossom
I am yours, captive
Peony
shame, bashfulness,
indignation, anger
Periwinkle, Blue
early friendship
Periwinkle, White
pleasures of memory
Peruvian Heliotrope
devoted to you
Petunia
never despair, anger,
resentment
Poinsettia
of good cheer

Poppy
eternal sleep, oblivion,
imagination, extravagance
Prickly Pear
satire
Primrose
can't live without you, early
youth, young love
Plum Tree
fidelity, promises
Roses
love, innocence, heavenly,
secrecy and silence, happiness,
believe me, jealousy, unity,
love at first sight, still love you
Rosebuds
youth, a heart innocent of love,
pure and lovely, girlhood
Rose leaf
you may hope
Rosemary
remembrance, commitment,
fidelity
Sage
wisdom, long life, domestic
virtue
Shamrock
lightheartedness
Snapdragon
no, deception, gracious lady,
presumption
Snowdrop
hope
Sorrel
with affection
Spanish Jasmine
sexy, sensual
Spearmint
warm feelings
Spider flower
elope with me

Sweet pea
goodbye, blissful pleasure,
thank you for a lovely time
Thyme
strength and courage
Tuberose
dangerous pleasure
Tulip
fame, charity, love, beautiful
eyes, hopeless love, believe me

Valerian
an accommodating disposition
Veronica
fidelity
Violet
modesty, faithfulness
Wallflower
fidelity in adversity

Valentine Delights Cookbook
A Collection of Valentine Recipes
Cookbook Delights Holiday Series - Book 2

Poetry

A Collection of Poetry with Valentine Themes

Table of Contents

The Valentine Spirit

Shedding inside and outside of the heart of love,
Waving the light inside the spiritual heart,
And inside the ways of life,

Heartiest love there is no tears as the sea,
Wishful ways of time there is no fear into the passion of
rivers,
Sweet dreams of time and love shall prevail,
Darkness and lightness collides to bring the road of love,

Softness the heartiest love of time shall reveal,
Explosion of time and life will lock the life of the heart,
Splendid the ways of time shall reveal the love in time,
Tears dry from the clouds onto the softness of the heart,
Kisses of love and romance shall realize the path of life,
Justice of time shall the love fall and rise again,

Only the two who love will rise above,
Upon the spirits will love only show emotion,
The softness of the heart will shed upon the face of life,
Rising above the heavens and the earth,
The heartiest man and woman rise in love,
Desiring the passion of life shall the roads of the Cupid
love combine,

The tulip of flowers move swiftly with the wind of time,
Let the tulip shine brighter with a kiss of love,
When the feeling of love rise above on the day of love,
The ones who love deeply in each other shall rise,
To be known as the Valentine spirit.

Karen Jean Matsko Hood ©2014
Published in *Valentine Delights Cookbook,* 2014
By Whispering Pine Press International, Inc., 2014

Brown Eyes

I remember his toffee eyes
friendly and warm,
full of life,
looking for fun.
Don't forget the smile,
that Cheshire-cat smirk.

Mischievous,
sensuous, lips
yearning to give.
Encore the brown eyes,
relaxed, affectionate,
ready to love
and to give again.

Memories abound.
His tender chocolate eyes,
soft lips of crimson.
How I miss his smile,
that impetuous grin.
The wish of
a kiss.

Karen Jean Matsko Hood ©2014
Published in *Valentine Delights Cookbook*, 2014
By Whispering Pine Press International, Inc., 2014

His Eyes

I felt his presence in the room,
Powerful, palpable presence in the room.
Ogle of his dark brown eyes,
Staring at me in the room.

A glance, a brief glance,
Is all that I would give
As I walked through the throng
In the now-claustrophobic room.

I often wonder,
If I paused,
And stopped, and looked,
And gave him back his eyes,

If that would cause
A transformation in myself,
A change that would turn about all time?
Instead, I vanish from the room.

Karen Jean Matsko Hood ©2014
Published in *Valentine Delights Cookbook,* 2014
By Whispering Pine Press International, Inc., 2014

I Love You

I love you more than bear grass,
      that blows in the wind.

I love you more than the fleabane,
      that undulates in the meadow.

I love you more than glacial streams
      that fall from clay cliffs.

I love you more than the blades of grass
      that wave in cool breezes.

I love you more than azure skies
      that drift across tall mountains.

My love grows far beyond the words
      written on the page.

My love for you is beauty beyond perfection;
      joy completes my craving.

Karen Jean Matsko Hood ©2014
Published in *Valentine Delights Cookbook,* 2014
By Whispering Pine Press International, Inc., 2014

My Love

My love is like a pink carnation,
That stands attached, fragrant in the wind.

My love is like the cinnamon spice,
That once lived atop the trunk

Of the tree that grows and still exists,
Only in a different form.

My love is like the sound of the cello,
Soothing with comfort to your soul.

My love is like the path to other galaxies,
Eternal and never ending.

Karen Jean Matsko Hood ©2014
Published in *Valentine Delights Cookbook,* 2014
By Whispering Pine Press International, Inc., 2014

Spilled Wine and Steel Drums

Wine spilled on the lace tablecloth
reminds me of you

and those fine meals we shared
alone together on the island.

Slowly sipping wine as we
savor Flounder Florentine.

Caribbean music serenades
us in the hushed background of ocean waves.

Fragrant blossoms perfume the air.
Sweet spilled red wine, and steel drums,

succulent Frangipani blossoms:
How delightful are the reminders of you.

Karen Jean Matsko Hood ©2014
Published in *Valentine Delights Cookbook,* 2014
By Whispering Pine Press International, Inc., 2014

Twinkle of Your Eye

Your chuckle makes me smile.
Your laughter brings me tears.

The twinkle in your eye
Is mystery for my soul.

I long for your embrace.
Your loving arms

Surround my heart,
And merriment dances once again.

Your voice I hear, although a whisper;
I long to feel your breath.

Karen Jean Matsko Hood ©2014
Published in *Valentine Delights Cookbook,* 2014
By Whispering Pine Press International, Inc., 2014

Beauty and Grace

Look out and see the beauty of the sun;
stand for a minute and enjoy your time.
Busy tasks wait for each item done.
Your clock of life is different than mine,
yet windows to our souls channel grace.
If only we could see spirits with our face!

Fear not the end of your heartbeat;
 tis' then that eternal life will begin.
All those gone before us we will meet
as long as we live in grace and avoid sin.
The staff will lead us to eternal grace,
if only we follow the light of His face.

Ask above for power to love;
we cannot use the excuse that we are weak.
Search and find the peace of the dove.
Yes, we must be humble; we cannot be meek.
We only have a short-term to live with grace,
to find the love that we all face.

Karen Jean Matsko Hood ©2014
Published in *Valentine Delights Cookbook,* 2014
By Whispering Pine Press International, Inc., 2014

Butterfly Blue

Butterfly, butterfly
Such beauty you show.

Butterfly, butterfly
Butterfly blue.

Wind and breeze
Grace that I know

Butterfly, butterfly
Butterfly blue.

Wind and breeze
Oceans I know

Butterfly, butterfly
Butterfly blue.

Wind and breeze
God's love I know.

Karen Jean Matsko Hood ©2014
Published in *Valentine Delights Cookbook,* 2014
By Whispering Pine Press International, Inc., 2014

Valentine Delights Cookbook
A Collection of Valentine Recipes
Cookbook Delights Holiday Series - Book 2

Valentine's Day Symbols

Valentine's Day Symbols

There are many types of Valentine symbols. All of them are an enjoyable way to decorate your Valentine gifts and meals. Valentine's Day is most closely associated with the mutual exchange of love notes in the form of "Valentines." Modern Valentine symbols include the heart-shaped outline and the figure of the winged Cupid, who is the Roman god of love. When he was shown originally, it was as a young man with a bow and arrows. But somehow, over years and years of time, the symbol changed from a young man to a cute, chubby baby. The myth is that Cupid is the son of Venus, who was the goddess of love and beauty, and so in his handsomeness, represents a symbol of love and passion. During the Victorian Era, however, it was not considered proper for women and children to think in such a manner. So, in order to make the day or celebration "more proper" Cupid was made less offensive by changing him from a handsome young man to the cute, chubby little baby with wings that we all know and love today.

Along with Cupid, other symbols of Valentine's Day are the colors of pink, red, and white, along with the shapes of hearts and arrows.

Pink is a symbol representing innocence, and red represents warmth or feelings, and is also the color of a human heart. Of course, most of us know that white is the symbol of purity or virginity.

The heart is a symbol of love, and when pierced by arrows, a broken love or rejection of love.

Valentine Delights Cookbook
A Collection of Valentine Recipes
Cookbook Delights Holiday Series - Book 2

Valentine Types

Valentine Types

Children and adults alike love to receive Valentine's Day cards. Most of us can remember the excitement of Valentine's Day as children. In elementary school they would have a special party just for the occasion. Mothers would bake cupcakes and decorate them with red and pink icing for their children to take to the class Valentine's Day party. No party was ever complete without the beloved Valentine box. Every child would decorate their own shoebox and cut a slit in the top to make it a Valentine mailbox of sorts. Children would work for hours the night before the great event, carefully writing out a Valentine for every single classmate. Of course, the cards with the most special messages were saved for the boy or girl of the child's affections. Excitement fills the air when children open their box of Valentines to read all of the messages. The tradition of exchanging cards for Valentine's Day is very longstanding, though the style and detail of these cards has evolved throughout the years.

During the Middle Ages, lovers sang Valentines to the one with whom they were enamored. It wasn't until the 1400s that handmade written Valentines appeared. These paper Valentines were given from one person to another when there were feelings of sentiment or romantic interest. The oldest existing Valentine on record dates back to the 1400s and is in a museum in London.

Valentines were originally handmade with different colors of paper, paints and inks, and many styles.

The most popular styles of Valentines over the years include Valentines which have had a loved one's name spelled out in the first lines, called an Acrostic Valentine. There have been Valentines made with bits of lace and colored threads and Valentines made by poking little holes in paper with needles which made the paper look "lacy." This type of Valentine is known as a "pinprick" Valentine.

In the early 1900s, several card companies got their beginnings and mass marketed cards began to be produced. This practice continues today, with Valentine's Day being responsible for the second largest card-producing day of the year.

Valentine Delights Cookbook
A Collection of Valentine Recipes
Cookbook Delights Holiday Series - Book 2

RECIPES

Valentine Delights Cookbook
A Collection of Valentine Recipes
Cookbook Delights Holiday Series - Book 2

Appetizers and Dips

Table of Contents

Page

Alaskan King Crab Cocktail

Our family loves crab, and this makes a delicious crab cocktail for special occasions.

Ingredients for crab cocktail:

> 3   c. Alaskan king crab meat
> 1½ c. red and yellow bell peppers, finely chopped
> 1½ c. celery, finely chopped
>   lettuce or spinach leaves, to line serving dish

Ingredients for cocktail sauce:

> 1   c. ketchup
> 2   Tbs. horseradish
> 2   tsp. hot sauce
> 1   tsp. white pepper
> 1   tsp. black pepper
> 1   tsp. salt
> ½   tsp. garlic powder
> 1   tsp. onion powder

Directions for cocktail sauce:

1. In small bowl, combine cocktail sauce ingredients; stir well.
2. Chill at least 1 hour.

Directions for crab cocktail:

1. To assemble the crab cocktail, line serving dish with lettuce or spinach leaves.
2. In medium bowl, combine crabmeat, red and yellow peppers, and celery together; stirring gently so that the large lumps of crabmeat are not broken.
3. Heap the crabmeat mixture on the greens.

4. Spoon cocktail sauce over salad; chill until ready to serve.

Yields: 12 servings.

Cherry Peanut Appetizer

This is an unusual spicy, cherry peanut appetizer, seasoned with cumin for an unexpected flavor treat.

Ingredients:

2   c. lightly salted peanuts
1   c. dried tart cherries
2   Tbs. hot sauce
1-2 tsp. canola oil
½   tsp. garlic powder
½   tsp. seasoning salt, or to taste
½   tsp. ground cumin
¼   tsp. ground red pepper (cayenne pepper), or to taste

Directions:

1. In medium bowl, combine peanuts and cherries.
2. In small bowl, combine hot sauce, garlic powder, seasoning salt, cumin, and red pepper; mix well.
3. Pour over peanut mixture, stir to coat.
4. In large skillet, over medium heat, heat oil.
5. Add peanut mixture; cook 3 to 4 minutes on medium-high, stirring constantly, until peanuts are light brown. Do not allow mixture to burn, adding more oil if needed.
6. Remove from heat.
7. Spread on parchment paper or aluminum foil to cool.
8. Store in an airtight container.

Yields: 3 cups.

Apple Turkey Rolls

This tasty turkey roll can be served as an appetizer or as a main dish.

Ingredients:

- 1 lb. ground turkey
- 2 c. apples, diced
- 2 c. bread crumbs
- 1 sm. onion, diced
- ½ tsp. sage
- ½ tsp. poultry seasoning
- ½ c. Cheddar cheese, grated

Directions:

1. Preheat oven to 350 degrees F.
2. On wax paper, flatten out ground turkey into a rectangle ½-inch thick.
3. In small bowl, combine apples, bread crumbs, sage, poultry seasoning, and onions; spread over meat.
4. Starting from the long end, roll as for jellyroll.
5. Place in 9 x 13-inch baking dish.
6. Bake 45 minutes.
7. During last 10 minutes of baking, sprinkle cheese over top of roll and finish baking.
8. Slice and serve on a serving platter.

Apple Fruit Cocktail Appetizer

For those looking for a sweet appetizer, this may be a recipe to spark the appetite.

Ingredients:

- 2 c. apple juice
- 1 Tbs. lemon juice

½ tsp. orange or lemon peel, grated
2 cinnamon sticks (3-inch)
2 red apples, cored, diced
1½ c. fresh pineapple, diced
1 orange, peeled, sectioned
   dash of salt

Directions:

1. In small saucepan, combine apple juice, lemon juice, orange or lemon peel, salt, and cinnamon sticks.
2. Bring to boil and simmer, uncovered, 10 minutes.
3. Cool slightly.
4. Remove cinnamon sticks.
5. Combine apples, pineapple, and orange.
6. Pour syrup over fruit and chill.

Harvest Apple Cheese Platter

This simple appetizer is very attractive with its wide varieties and colors, tastes, textures, and selection of cheeses.

Ingredients:

Golden Delicious apples
Granny Smith apples
Red Delicious apples
choice of assorted cheeses: Cheddar, blue, Brie, Edam, Swiss, Colby, Monterey jack, etc.

Directions:

1. Slice or quarter apples and cheeses, or if desired, set out apple cutters and cheese knives.
2. Arrange apples and cheeses on attractive cheese board or platter; serve.

Delicious Apple Spread Tray

This mixed spread is easily prepared and is great served with crackers, pita bread, or slices of French bread.

Ingredients:

> 1 Tbs. caraway seeds
> 3 oz. cream cheese, softened
> ½ c. butter, softened
> ½ c. cottage cheese
> ½ tsp. hot pepper sauce
> ¼ c. green onion, finely chopped
> 1 sm. garlic clove, minced
> ½ lb. cooked ham, chopped into sm. pieces

Directions:

1. In blender or food processor, process caraway seeds.
2. Add rest of ingredients; blend well.
3. Chill spread for several hours or overnight.
4. Serve spread on apple slices, or on your favorite cracker, alongside apple wedges.

Apple Dip

This is an easy-to-make dip for slices of apples that makes a nice alternative to caramel dip. This makes an attractive presentation of red and white for a Valentine's Day appetizer.

Ingredients:

> 1 pkg. cream cheese (8 oz.)
> ½ c. brown sugar
> 1 Tbs. vanilla extract
>   red apples, sliced

Directions:

1. In medium mixing bowl, combine cream cheese, brown sugar, and vanilla until thoroughly blended.
2. If mixture is too runny for your taste, add small amount of brown sugar to mixture.
3. If mixture is too thick for your taste, add small amount of vanilla extract.
4. Wash your apple, dip, and enjoy.

Artichoke Crab Dip

This is a flavorful and easy-to-make dip that is best with French bread. Be sure you make extra because it will disappear quickly.

Ingredients:

1 can artichoke hearts (14 oz.)
1 sm. can crab meat
1 c. mayonnaise
1 c. Parmesan cheese
1 pinch garlic powder
   sliced French bread, toasted, buttered

Directions:

1. Preheat oven to 350 degrees F.
2. Drain artichokes and cut into quarters.
3. In medium bowl, combine mayonnaise, garlic powder, and cheese; mix well.
4. Fold in artichokes and crabmeat.
5. Place mixture in glass pie dish.
6. Bake 25 to 30 minutes, or until hot and bubbly.
7. Serve warm with slices of toasted and buttered French bread.

Cranberry Veggie Balls

These are wonderful vegetarian meatballs with a sweet and sour sauce. They're simple to make, and they disappear very quickly. Make these for Valentine holiday parties. If you don't have veggie burger patties, you may use textured vegetable protein (TVP), which is available at most health food stores.

Ingredients:

    4   eggs, beaten
    1   c. flaked corn cereal, crushed
    ⅓   c. chili sauce
    1   Tbs. soy sauce
    1½ tsp. dried parsley flakes
    2   Tbs. dried onion flakes
    8   vegetarian burger patties
    4   oz. buttery round crackers, crumbled
    1   pkg. cream cheese, softened (8 oz.)
    1   c. walnuts, chopped
    1   can jellied cranberry sauce (16 oz.)
    1   c. Russian style salad dressing
    2   tsp. brown sugar
    1   Tbs. lemon juice

Directions:

    1. Preheat oven to 350 degrees F.
    2. Lightly spray two baking sheets with nonstick cooking spray.
    3. In medium bowl, combine eggs, cereal, chili sauce, soy sauce, parsley flakes, onion flakes, burgers, crackers, cream cheese, and walnuts.
    4. Shape into 72 1-inch meatballs.
    5. Arrange on prepared baking sheets.
    6. Bake 20 to 25 minutes, or until meatballs are cooked through.

7. In large saucepan, combine cranberry sauce, Russian dressing, brown sugar, and lemon juice.
8. Cook, stirring frequently until the cranberry sauce is melted.
9. Add meatballs and heat through.
10. Serve with appetizer toothpicks, if desired.

Caviar Heart Kisses

This is a nice appetizer for a holiday, especially when shared with special company.

Ingredients:

1 sm. cucumber, scrubbed, trimmed
⅓ c. sour cream
1 tsp. dried dill weed
1 jar red salmon caviar
8 thin slices whole wheat bread
   black pepper, ground, to taste
   fresh dill sprigs, for garnish
   butter

Directions:

1. Slice cucumbers into ¼-inch rounds.
2. In small bowl, combine sour cream, dried dill, and black pepper.
3. Place 1 teaspoon of sour cream mixture on each cucumber slice.
4. Garnish each with ½ teaspoon caviar and a dill sprig.
5. Cut bread slices into heart shapes with a cookie cutter.
6. Toast bread slices and butter.
7. Place cucumber slices in center of serving plate and surround with toast hearts.

Feta Apple Pimento Blend

This makes an interesting, colorful appetizer spread with a nutritious blend of fruit, vegetables, and cheese.

Ingredients:

    4   oz. pimentos, diced, drained
    1½ med. red apples, cored, peeled, diced
    1   med. carrot, peeled, shredded
    8   oz. Feta cheese, crumbled
    ½   c. sour cream
    ¼   c. black olives, pitted, finely chopped
    1   Tbs. parsley, chopped

Directions:

1. In large bowl, combine pimentos, apples, and carrots; mix well.
2. In small bowl, combine cheese and sour cream.
3. Stir into apples and carrots until well blended.
4. Chill until ready to serve.
5. Serve on bagels, quartered pita rounds or crackers, topped with olives and parsley.

Cheese Squares

This makes a nice appetizer that can be prepared ahead of time and then baked as needed.

Ingredients:

    2   lg. loaves white bread, sliced
    16 oz. cheese spread
    3   Tbs. Beau Monde seasoning
    1   Tbs. hot sauce
    1   lb. butter
         hot sauce, to taste

Directions:

1. Trim crusts off all the bread.
2. In small bowl, mix together remaining ingredients very thoroughly.
3. Spread mixture on 3 slices of bread.
4. Stack slices one on top of the other.
5. Cut stack into quarters.
6. Repeat with remaining bread slices and cheese mixture.
7. Freeze stacks on a baking sheet.
8. Store frozen in plastic bags until ready for use.
9. Note: They may be kept frozen up to 3 months.
10. When ready to use, bake stacks on a greased baking sheet for 8 minutes at 400 degrees F.

Valentine's Day Salmon Pâté

Pâté makes a great appetizer for Valentine's Day. This is very easy to prepare and delicious with the salmon and cream cheese.

Ingredients:

1 pkg. cream cheese (8 oz.)
1 tsp. horseradish
1 Tbs. lemon juice
1 c. salmon, flaked
2 tsp. onion, minced
2 Tbs. fresh parsley, chopped
½ tsp. liquid smoke
    fresh parsley sprigs, for garnish

Directions:

1. In medium bowl, blend together, cream cheese, horseradish, lemon juice, salmon, onion, parsley, and liquid smoke.
2. Transfer mixture to a serving bowl; garnish with fresh parsley sprigs.
3. Serve with party rye bread or crackers.

Dill and Salmon Stuffed Eggs

Salmon, dill, and eggs make a great combination, as well as an easy-to-make appetizer.

Ingredients:

    12 eggs
    6 Tbs. mayonnaise
    8 oz. salmon, slivered
    ⅛ tsp. mustard powder
    1 tsp. lemon juice
    ½ tsp. fresh dill weed, finely minced
    24 tiny sprigs of fresh dill weed (½-inch long)

Directions:

1. Put eggs into a saucepan and cover with water.
2. Bring eggs to a boil, and boil gently for 20 to 30 minutes.
3. Cool eggs by running cold water over them.
4. Cut each egg into even halves.
5. Remove and reserve the yolks.
6. Cut 24 slivers of salmon to be reserved for garnishing the egg.
7. Finely chop the remaining salmon.
8. In medium bowl, mash together chopped salmon, egg yolks, mayonnaise, mustard powder, minced dill weed, and lemon until well mixed.
9. Stuff egg white halves with egg yolk and salmon mixture.
10. Garnish with slivers of salmon and dill weed sprigs.

Did You Know? . . . .

Did you know that in Victorian times it was considered bad luck to sign a Valentine's Day card?

Valentine Delights Cookbook
A Collection of Valentine Recipes
Cookbook Delights Holiday Series - Book 2

Beverages

Table of Contents

Almond Cocoa

The flavor of almonds enhances the warming flavor of hot cocoa.

Ingredients:

 3 Tbs. sugar
 3 Tbs. unsweetened cocoa powder
 4 c. milk
 1 tsp. vanilla extract
 12 drops almond extract

Directions:

1. In medium saucepan, stir together sugar and cocoa powder.
2. Gradually stir in milk until smooth.
3. Heat over medium heat until hot, stirring all the while to prevent scorching.
4. Remove from heat; stir in vanilla and almond extract.

Austrian Chocolate Cup

Try this delectable combination of cinnamon, orange flavor, and chocolate. It is delicious.

Ingredients:

 16 oz. semi-sweet chocolate, broken in pieces
 5   tsp. orange peel, finely grated
 1¼ tsp. ground cinnamon
 8   c. milk, divided
 1¼ c. sweetened whipping cream
 8   cinnamon sticks (3-inch pieces)
     chocolate, grated

Directions:

1. In medium saucepan, combine chocolate, orange peel, cinnamon, and 3 tablespoons of milk.
2. Over medium heat, stir until chocolate melts.
3. Add remaining milk and heat through gently until piping hot, stirring frequently.
4. In small bowl, with electric mixer, whip cream until soft peaks form.
5. Pour hot chocolate into mugs or heatproof glasses.
6. Top with whipped cream.
7. Sprinkle with grated chocolate, and add a cinnamon stick to each one for stirring.

Yields: 8 servings.

Cherry Berry Ice Cream Drink

This makes an attractive, easy-to-make, pink ice cream drink.

Ingredients:

4 cherries
4 blueberries
2 Tbs. raspberry syrup
2 c. prepared lemonade
2 scoops vanilla ice cream

Directions:

1. In two tall glasses, place 2 cherries and 2 blueberries each.
2. Pour 1 tablespoon raspberry syrup over berries in each glass.
3. Gently pour in the lemonade, top each glass with a scoop of ice cream.

Cherry Cider

Add some romantic, spiced cherry apple cider to your Valentine's Day dinner. Spiced cider is always a delicious drink.

Ingredients:

> 2 qt. apple cider
> 1 cinnamon stick (3-inch)
> 2 c. sweet cherry juice

Directions:

1. In large saucepan, bring cider; cherry juice, and cinnamon stick to a boil.
2. Reduce heat and simmer 15 minutes.
3. Serve warm.

Yields: 8 servings.

Cherry Ice Cream Shake

Cherries make an ice cream shake taste great, and pink is a perfect color for Valentine's Day.

Ingredients:

> 12 oz. dark sweet cherries, pitted, drained
> 2 c. vanilla ice cream

Directions:

1. In blender, combine cherries and vanilla ice cream.
2. Blend until mixture is smooth and creamy.
3. Pour into two 14-ounce glasses and serve immediately.

Cherry Spiced Cider

Our family loves spiced ciders, and this makes a tasty drink with the addition of maraschino cherries. This tasty beverage is a delicious treat for Valentine's Day.

Ingredients:

½ c. maraschino cherry juice
1 qt. apple cider
¾ c. orange juice
1 stick cinnamon (3-inch)
1 strip orange peel (½ x 3-inch)
3 whole cloves
3 whole allspice
16 red maraschino cherries
8 orange slice halves

Directions:

1. In large saucepan, combine cherry juice, apple cider, orange juice, cinnamon sticks, orange peel, cloves, and allspice; bring to boil.
2. Reduce heat; simmer 15 minutes.
3. Strain out cinnamon sticks, orange peel, cloves, and allspice.
4. Place 2 maraschino cherries and 1 orange slice half in each of six mugs.
5. Pour ⅔ cup spiced cider over cherries.
6. Serve warm.
7. Note: Spiced cider can be prepared in advance and reheated just before serving.

Did You Know? . . . .

Did you know that 15 percent of U.S. women send themselves flowers on Valentine's Day?

Chocolate Mint Coffee

Give this as a gift, or store in your refrigerator for adding to your next cup of coffee. It makes a delicious drink.

Ingredients:

⅔ c. instant coffee
1 Tbs. chocolate extract
1 tsp. mint extract
1 tsp. vanilla extract

Directions:

1. Place coffee in a blender or food processor.
2. In a cup, combine extracts.
3. With processor running, add extracts.
4. Stop and scrape sides of container with spatula.
5. Process 10 seconds longer.
6. Use by teaspoonfuls to taste.
7. Store in cool place.

Cranberry Raspberry Punch

This makes a festive, colorful punch to serve on Valentine's Day.

Ingredients:

2 qt. raspberry sherbet
1½ qt. vanilla ice cream
1 qt. cranberry cocktail
1 qt. lemon lime soda

Directions:

1. In large bowl, soften sherbet and ice cream.
2. Add 1 cup of juice; mix.
3. Add remaining juice; blend well.
4. Just before serving, add lemon lime soda.

Chocolate Mint Sipper

For those who enjoy the combination of chocolate and mint, this is a soothing drink.

Ingredients:

- 1   c. chocolate milk
- 2-3 peppermint hard candies, finely crushed
- 2   Tbs. marshmallow crème
- 2   tsp. chocolate syrup

Directions:

1. In small saucepan, combine chocolate milk, peppermint candies, marshmallow crème, and chocolate syrup.
2. Cook and stir over medium heat until mixture is heated through and candies are dissolved.

Shirley Temple

Children and adults alike seem to enjoy this classic non-alcoholic drink. We serve it on special occasions and it makes an easy Valentine's Day drink.

Ingredients:

- 20 oz. ginger ale
- 4   oz. grenadine
    ice cubes
    maraschino cherries, to garnish

Directions:

1. Divide grenadine evenly amongst four highball glasses, then fill each glass with ice cubes.
2. Add ginger ale over ice.
3. Garnish with a cherry.

Chocolate Espresso Cooler

Try this wonderful drink while waiting for your meal to finish cooking, or as an after dinner drink if the weather is warm.

Ingredients:

2   c. cold espresso blend coffee
2   c. cold milk
2-3 heaping tsp. sweetened chocolate milk mix
1   tsp. vanilla extract
1   c. sweetened whipped cream

Directions:

1. In blender, place milk mix.
2. Add 2 cups milk and blend.
3. Add coffee, cocoa, and vanilla; blend 5 seconds.
4. Pour over ice in tall glasses.
5. Top each with a dollop of sweetened whipped cream.

Strawberry Julius

This strawberry drink can be made year round with frozen strawberries stashed in the freezer.

Ingredients:

10 oz. frozen strawberries
1   c. water
1   c. milk
2 Tbs. sugar
1   tsp. vanilla extract
11 ice cubes

Directions:

1. In blender, combine all ingredients except ice.
2. Cover and blend, quickly adding ice cubes one at a time, until smooth.
3. Serve immediately.

Yields: 6 servings.

Hot Cocoa

Nothing is more soothing on a cold day than hot cocoa. Serve with your choice of marshmallows, sweetened whipped cream, or a sprinkle of cinnamon.

Ingredients:

½ c. unsweetened cocoa powder
½ c. sugar
3 c. water
2 tsp. vanilla extract
2 qt. milk
  dash of salt

Directions:

1. In small saucepan, blend cocoa, sugar, and salt; gradually stir in enough water to make a smooth paste.
2. Stir in rest of water and vanilla.
3. Bring mixture to a boil; simmer 10 minutes.
4. Meanwhile, scald milk over low heat.
5. Stir in boiled cocoa mixture.
6. Cover.
7. Reduce heat to lowest temperature.
8. Simmer for 30 minutes to mellow.

Creamy Raspberry Sipper

This recipe makes a refreshing, cold drink.

Ingredients:

    1¼ c. fresh raspberries
    1¼ c. unsweetened white grape juice
    1½ c. raspberry sherbet
    ¼ c. water
    1   Tbs. lemon juice
    10 ice cubes
        fresh mint sprigs, for garnish

Directions:

1. In blender, combine raspberries and grape juice; cover and process until smooth.
2. Add sherbet, water, and lemon juice; cover and process until smooth.
3. Add ice cubes; process until frothy.
4. Garnish with fresh mint sprigs.

Easy Raspberry Lemonade

This recipe makes a light and fruity drink.

Ingredients:

    1   can frozen raspberry lemonade concentrate (12 oz.)
    3   c. water
    ¾   tsp. lime juice
    1   can or bottle lemon lime soda
    1   c. ice, crushed
    1   c. fresh raspberries, for garnish
    1   c. fresh mint, for garnish

Directions:

1. In large punch bowl, combine concentrate, water, and lime juice.
2. Stir in lemon lime soda and crushed ice.
3. Garnish with raspberries and a few mint leaves.

Valentine Delights Cookbook
A Collection of Valentine Recipes
Cookbook Delights Holiday Series - Book 2

Breads and Rolls

Table of Contents

Page

Cherry Heart Twist

This is an attractive and delicious bread, and it looks inviting served at a buffet or brunch.

Ingredients:

1 pkg. yeast
⅓ c. sugar
⅔ c. water, warm
1 c. hazelnuts, toasted, skinned
3 c. flour
1 tsp. salt
¼ c. butter, unsalted, room temperature
1 egg
¾ c. dried cherries
  icing

Directions:

1. Preheat oven to 350 degrees F.
2. Spread hazelnuts on baking sheet.
3. Bake 8 to10 minutes, or until toasted.
4. Rub hot hazelnuts in a clean kitchen towel to remove the skins.
5. In small cup, dissolve yeast and 1 teaspoon sugar in warm water; let sit until foamy, 5 to 10 minutes.
6. Place half of hazelnuts in blender or food processor.
7. Whirl until chopped; remove and reserve.
8. Place remaining nuts and remaining sugar in blender or food processor; whirl until finely ground.
9. Add flour, salt, and butter.
10. With blender or processor running, add egg and yeast mix.
11. Whirl until mix forms a ball; whirl 30 seconds more to knead.
12. Place dough in a lightly greased bowl, turn to coat.
13. Cover with a damp cloth.
14. Let rise in warm place, away from drafts, until double in bulk, about 1½ hours.
15. Punch dough down.
16. On lightly floured surface, knead in reserved nuts and cherries; divide the dough in half.
17. Roll each half into a 24-inch long rope.

18. Twist the ropes together.
19. On a greased baking sheet, form the braided loaf into a heart shape; cover with a damp cloth.
20. Let rise in a warm place, away from drafts, until double in bulk, about 1 hour.
21. Preheat oven to 350 degrees F.
22. Bake 25 to 30 minutes, or until golden brown.
23. Cool bread on wire rack.
24. In medium bowl, combine 1½ cups powdered sugar and 2 to 3 tablespoons milk until blended and good icing consistency; divide icing in half.
25. Tint one half with red food coloring.
26. Drizzle or pipe red and white icings in heart shapes over bread.

Strawberry Nut Bread

Strawberries make a great fruit and nut bread, and this is a nice bread to serve as a snack or for brunch.

Ingredients:

3   c. flour
2   c. sugar
1   tsp. baking soda
1   tsp. salt
1   tsp. almond extract
1   pkg. frozen strawberries, thawed, drained
4   eggs, lightly beaten
1¼ c. canola oil
1   c. walnuts or pecans, chopped

Directions:

1. Preheat oven to 350 degrees F.
2. Lightly grease and flour two loaf pans.
3. In large bowl, combine flour, sugar, baking soda, and salt.
4. In medium bowl, mash strawberries well.
5. Add eggs, almond extract, and oil.
6. Combine with flour mixture, mixing well.
7. Pour into prepared pans.
8. Bake 50 to 60 minutes, or until golden brown and inserted toothpick comes out clean.

Cherry Cheddar Bread

This combination of sweet cherries, Cheddar, and chopped nuts makes great-tasting bread.

Ingredients:

2½ c. flour
½ c. sugar
½ c. brown sugar
3 tsp. baking powder
1 tsp. salt
1¼ c. milk
1 egg
3 Tbs. canola oil
1¼ c. fresh sweet cherries, pitted, coarsely chopped
1¼ c. Cheddar cheese, grated
1¼ c. walnuts or pecans, chopped

Directions:

1. Preheat oven to 350 degrees F.
2. Lightly grease a 9¼ x 5¼ x 2¾-inch loaf pan.
3. In large bowl, combine flour, sugar, brown sugar, baking powder, and salt.
4. In small bowl, combine milk, egg, and oil; pour over dry ingredients and stir just enough to dampen.
5. Gently fold in cherries, cheese, and nuts.
6. Pour into prepared pan.
7. Bake 55 to 65 minutes, or until inserted toothpick comes out clean.
8. Cool on rack 10 minutes; remove from pan.
9. Cool completely before serving.

Did You Know? . . . .

Did you know that about 3 percent of pet owners will give Valentine's Day gifts to their pets?

Cherry Muffins

Dried cherries are excellent in muffins, and the almond flavoring adds a special taste.

Ingredients:

¾ c. dried cherries, coarsely chopped
2 Tbs. almond flavoring
2 c. flour
3 tsp. baking powder
½ tsp. salt
¼ c. sugar
1 egg
1 c. milk
¼ c. butter, melted

Directions:

1. Preheat oven to 400 degrees.
2. Place cherries in a small ovenproof bowl or pan.
3. Stir in almond flavoring and cover.
4. Place in oven for 5 to 10 minutes so cherries will puff up and absorb liquid.
5. Stir once or twice and set aside.
6. Lightly grease a muffin tin.
7. Reduce oven temperature to 375 degrees F.
8. In large bowl, sift together dry ingredients.
9. In a separate bowl, beat together egg, milk, and butter.
10. Quickly fold in dry ingredients; stir in cherries.
11. Spoon into prepared muffin pan, filling each cup ⅔ full.
12. Bake 20 to 25 minutes.

Yields: 12 muffins.

Chocolate Brownie Bread

This makes delicious bread for a snack and a great lunchbox treat.

Ingredients:

- 4 sq. unsweetened baking chocolate
- ½ c. butter
- 1 c. sugar
- 1 c. brown sugar, firmly packed
- 2 eggs, lightly beaten
- 1 c. sour cream
- 1 tsp. vanilla extract
- 1½ c. flour
- 2 tsp. baking powder
- ¼ tsp. baking soda
- 1 c. walnuts, finely chopped

Directions:

1. Preheat oven to 350 degrees F.
2. Grease and flour a 9 x 5-inch loaf pan.
3. Over medium heat, melt butter and chocolate together until completely melted, stirring often.
4. Add sugars; mix well.
5. Blend in eggs, sour cream, and vanilla.
6. Add flour, baking powder, and baking soda; mix well.
7. Stir in walnuts.
8. Spread batter into prepared pan.
9. Bake 60 to 70 minutes, or until inserted toothpick comes out clean.
10. Cool in pan for 10 minutes.
11. Remove from pan to wire rack.
12. Cool completely before cutting.

Cranberry Chocolate Bread

Cranberries and chocolate combined make great-tasting homemade bread. You may want to double the recipe and keep one loaf in the freezer.

Ingredients:

- 1 c. semi-sweet chocolate chips
- 1 c. fresh or frozen cranberries, coarsely chopped
- ½ c. pecans, chopped
- 2 tsp. orange peel, freshly grated
- 2 c. flour
- 1 c. sugar
- 1½ tsp. baking powder
- ½ tsp. baking soda
- ½ tsp. salt
- 2 Tbs. butter
- ¾ c. orange juice
- 1 egg, slightly beaten

Directions:

1. Preheat oven to 350 degrees F.
2. Grease and flour three 5¾ x 3¼ x 2-inch loaf pans.
3. In small bowl, stir together chocolate chips, cranberries, pecans, and orange peel; set aside.
4. In large bowl, stir together flour, sugar, baking powder, baking soda, and salt.
5. With pastry blender, cut in shortening until mixture resembles coarse crumbs.
6. Stir in orange juice, egg, and chocolate chip mixture just until moistened; divide evenly between prepared pans.
7. Bake 40 to 45 minutes, or until inserted toothpick comes out clean.
8. Cool 15 minutes in pans; remove to wire rack.
9. Cool completely; if desired, drizzle with glaze.

Cranberry Banana Bread

The red cranberries and bananas add flavor, moisture, and a beautiful color to this irresistible bread.

Ingredients:

2⅔ c. sugar, divided
1   c. water
4   c. fresh cranberries
1¾ c. flour, sifted
½   tsp. salt
2   tsp. baking powder
¼   tsp. baking soda
⅓   c. butter, melted
2   eggs, beaten
1   c. walnuts, chopped
1   c. banana, mashed
¼   c. cranberry juice, reserved from cooked berries
2   Tbs. powdered sugar

Directions:

1. Preheat oven to 350 degrees F.
2. Lightly grease and flour a 9 x 5 x 3-inch loaf pan.
3. In large saucepan, bring 2 cups sugar and water to a boil, stirring to dissolve the sugar.
4. Add berries; over low heat, simmer 10 minutes, or until berries pop open; cool.
5. Drain the berries, reserving the juice, then measure 1 cup of berries for use in the bread.
6. In medium bowl, sift together flour, salt, baking powder, and baking soda.
7. In large bowl, combine remaining sugar, butter, eggs, walnuts, banana, and the cup of berries.
8. Add flour mixture to berry mixture, stirring together until blended.
9. Pour into prepared pan.
10. Bake 1 hour, or until inserted toothpick comes out clean.

11. In small saucepan, combine reserved cranberry juice and powdered sugar.
12. Stir over low heat until heated through.
13. Poke a few holes in the baked loaf with the handle of a wooden spoon; pour the topping over the bread.
14. Cool 10 minutes in the pan.
15. Turn out on a rack, turn right-side up immediately.
16. Cool completely; wrap in foil and store for 1 day before slicing.

Raspberry Bread

Raspberries make this bread taste like a bit of summer all year round. Don't be afraid to double the recipe, as it also freezes well.

Ingredients:

3　c. flour
2　c. sugar
3　tsp. cinnamon
1　tsp. baking soda
1　tsp. salt
20　oz. frozen raspberries, thawed, drained
4　eggs, beaten
1¼ c. canola oil
1　c. walnuts or pecans, chopped

Directions:

1. Preheat oven to 350 degrees F.
2. Lightly grease two loaf pans.
3. In large bowl, mix flour, sugar, cinnamon, baking soda, salt, and nuts together.
4. In large bowl, mash raspberries well.
5. Add eggs and oil.
6. Combine with flour mixture; mix well.
7. Pour into prepared pans.
8. Bake 1 hour, or until inserted toothpick comes out clean.

Dried Cherry Scones

There is nothing quite as good as warm scones, fresh out of the oven.

Ingredients:

2 c. cake flour
2 c. flour
4 tsp. baking powder
½ c. sugar
¼ tsp. salt
⅞ c. butter, chilled, cut into sm. pieces
1 lg. egg, beaten
¾ c. milk
1 c. dried cherries
  light cream
  sugar

Directions:

1. Preheat oven to 375 degrees F.
2. Lightly grease a baking sheet.
3. In food processor, combine cake flour, flour, baking powder, sugar, and salt.
4. Add butter, egg, and milk; pulse until dough starts to come together.
5. Turn dough onto a lightly floured surface and knead lightly, folding in dried cherries at the same time.
6. Gently form dough into a smooth 10-inch circle about 1-inch thick.
7. With a large knife, cut dough into 12 pie-shaped wedges.
8. Brush each lightly with cream, then dust with sugar.
9. Place on prepared baking sheet.
10. Bake 20 minutes, or until lightly browned.

Raspberry Muffins

These are absolutely delicious muffins bursting with flavor. Serve them hot out of the oven with butter and extra raspberry preserves, if you prefer.

Ingredients:

½ c. butter
1½ c. sugar
2   eggs
2   c. flour
2   tsp. baking powder
½   tsp. salt
2   c. fresh raspberries
½   c. milk
1   tsp. vanilla extract
    sugar, for topping

Directions:

1. Preheat oven to 375 degrees F.
2. Lightly grease or paper-line muffin cups.
3. In large bowl, cream butter and sugar together.
4. Add eggs, one at a time, mixing until blended.
5. In small bowl, sift together flour, baking powder, and salt.
6. Add to butter and sugar mixture, alternating with the milk and vanilla.
7. In small bowl, mash ½ cup raspberries; stir into batter.
8. Add remaining whole berries (coating the berries with some flour will help to prevent them from sinking to the bottom of the bowl).
9. Fill muffin cups just about full and sprinkle with sugar.
10. Bake 25 to 30 minutes.

Strawberry Almond Bread

This is a delicious strawberry and almond nut bread, which also freezes well.

Ingredients:

2 eggs
½ c. canola oil
1 c. sugar
10 oz. frozen sliced strawberries, thawed
1½ c. flour
1½ tsp. cinnamon
½ tsp. baking soda
¼ tsp. salt
1 c. almonds, chopped

Directions:

1. Preheat oven to 350 degrees F.
2. Lightly grease and flour an 8-inch loaf pan.
3. In small bowl, beat eggs until fluffy.
4. Add oil, sugar, and strawberries.
5. In large mixing bowl, sift together flour, cinnamon, baking soda, and salt.
6. Stir in strawberry mixture, mixing until well blended, and then stir in almonds.
7. Scrape dough into prepared pan.
8. Bake 1 hour and 10 minutes, or until done.
9. Cool in pan, 10 minutes; turn out onto rack to cool.

Raspberry Streusel Muffins

These muffins are absolutely scrumptious! Serve them warm, and everyone will ask for more.

Ingredients for muffins:

1½ c. whole wheat flour
¼ c. sugar

¼ c. brown sugar, packed
2 tsp. baking powder
¼ tsp. salt
1 tsp. cinnamon
1 lg. egg, lightly beaten
½ c. butter, melted
½ c. milk
1¼ c. raspberries, fresh or frozen
1 tsp. lemon zest, grated

Ingredients for topping:

½ c. pecans, chopped
½ c. brown sugar, packed
¼ c. whole wheat flour
1 tsp. cinnamon
1 tsp. lemon zest
2 Tbs. butter, melted

Directions for muffins:

1. In medium bowl, sift together flour, sugar, brown sugar, baking powder, salt, and cinnamon.
2. Make a well in the center.
3. Place the egg, butter, and milk in the well.
4. Stir with a wooden spoon just until the ingredients are combined.
5. Lightly stir in raspberries and lemon zest.

Directions for topping:

1. Preheat oven to 350 degrees F.
2. Grease or paper-line muffin cups.
3. Fill muffin cups ¾ full.
4. In small bowl, combine pecans, brown sugar, flour, cinnamon, and lemon zest together.
5. Pour in melted butter and combine with a fork until crumbly.
6. Sprinkle evenly over the tops of each muffin.
7. Bake 20 to 25 minutes.
8. Cool on racks.

Strawberry Bagels

These bagels are sweet and chewy, and you may substitute the dried fruit for any other of your preference for a change of pace.

Ingredients:

2 c. water, warm
4 Tbs. sugar
4½ tsp. yeast
5-6 c. flour
2 tsp. salt
1 c. dried strawberries
2 tsp. strawberry, raspberry, or cherry flavoring
2 Tbs. cornmeal, for baking sheet
1 egg, mixed with 1 Tbs. water, for egg wash

Directions:

1. In small bowl, combine the flavoring and berries; set aside.
2. In large bowl, mix yeast, sugar, and warm water; let sit for 5 minutes, or until bubbly.
3. Add berry mixture to the yeast mixture.
4. With a wooden spoon, mix in 4 to 5 cups of flour.
5. When dough gets stiff, turn out onto a lightly flour surface and knead for 5 minutes, adding flour as needed.
6. Place dough in a lightly greased large bowl; cover with damp cloth and let rise until double in size.
7. Punch down dough and divide into 12 balls.
8. Shape each ball into a bagel by placing a hole in the center of each with your thumb; spin the dough on your finger to widen the hole.
9. After shaping bagels, place on parchment paper to rise for 15 minutes; covering with a tea towel.
10. In large pot, bring 12 cups of water and one tablespoon of sugar to a rolling boil.
11. Boil bagels for 2 to 3 minutes on each side for a total of 5 minutes.
12. Remove bagels from water with a slotted spoon.

13. Place on paper towels to drain.
14. Sprinkle cornmeal on the same parchment paper and arrange boiled bagels.
15. Brush each boiled bagel with an egg wash.
16. Bake in preheated oven at 400 degrees F. for 25 to 30 minutes, or until golden brown.
17. Remove from oven and place on wire rack to cool, or serve warm from the oven.

Yields: 12 bagels.

Strawberry Bran Muffins

These muffins are delicious, nutritious, and wonderful served right from the oven with butter.

Ingredients:

1 c. flour
½ c. sugar
1½ tsp. baking powder
¼ tsp. salt
1 c. bran cereal
1 c. milk
1 egg
3 Tbs. canola oil
¾ c. strawberry jam

Directions:

1. Preheat oven to 400 degrees F.
2. Lightly grease or paper-line muffin cups.
3. In medium bowl, sift together flour, sugar, baking powder, and salt; set aside.
4. In large bowl, measure bran and milk; mix well.
5. Let stand 3 minutes, or until most of moisture is taken up.
6. Add egg and oil, mixing well.
7. Add flour mixture, stirring until just combined.
8. Spoon batter evenly into prepared muffin cups.
9. Make deep indentation in top of batter of each muffin; fill each with 1 teaspoon jam.
10. Bake 20 minutes, or until golden brown.

Heavenly Chocolate Bread

This delicious chocolate bread is sweet, but not too sweet, and moist.

Ingredients:

4   oz. unsweetened chocolate or 12 Tbs. cocoa powder
½   c. butter
4   eggs
⅔   c. honey
2   c. potatoes, mashed
½   c. brandy, rum, orange juice, or a mixture
2   tsp. vanilla extract (optional)
2   tsp. orange zest
2¼ c. flour
4   tsp. baking powder
1   tsp. salt

Directions:

1. Preheat oven to 350 degrees F.
2. Lightly grease three 7 x 3-inch loaf pans.
3. In a microwaveable bowl, melt chocolate and butter; mix together.
4. In another bowl, beat eggs until frothy.
5. Add honey, mashed potatoes, alcohol and/or juice, vanilla, and orange zest.
6. Stir in chocolate-butter mixture.
7. In separate bowl, mix together flour, baking powder, and salt.
8. Stir 2 cups of flour mixture into wet mixture. The mixture should be a heavy batter. If too thin, add rest of the flour mixture and stir until everything is moistened.
9. Pour batter into prepared pans.
10. Bake on center rack, 40 minutes, or until inserted toothpick comes out clean.

Valentine Delights Cookbook
A Collection of Valentine Recipes
Cookbook Delights Holiday Series - Book 2

Breakfasts

Table of Contents

Page

Apple Sausage Oven Pancake

This is an interesting and very tasty pancake. Children and adults alike enjoy the medley of flavors. Serve hot with maple syrup.

Ingredients:

4 lg. sausage patties, select your favorite
2 red apples, cored, sliced ¼-inch thick
2 Tbs. brown sugar
1 tsp. cinnamon
4 eggs
1¼ c. milk
1 c. flour
½ c. butter, divided

Directions:

1. Preheat oven to 350 degrees F.
2. In large skillet, break up and sauté sausage patties until browned; remove and drain on paper towels.
3. Pour off drippings from skillet; toss in ¼ cup of butter and top with apple slices.
4. Sprinkle with sugar and cinnamon.
5. Sauté 1 to 2 minutes until apples just lose their crispness; set aside.
6. Place remaining butter in a well seasoned 10 or 12-inch iron skillet.
7. Heat skillet in oven until bubbly and hot; remove from oven.
8. While skillet is heating, in a blender, combine eggs and milk; pulse several times, adding flour slowly while blending, and blend until all batter is smooth.
9. Quickly arrange sausage in hot skillet; cover with sautéed apples, distributing evenly.
10. Pour mixture over sausage-apple mixture.

11. Return to oven.
12. Bake 15 to 20 minutes, or until golden brown.
13. Tip out of pan onto serving platter, dust with powdered sugar.
14. Cut into pie-shaped wedges.

Caramel Breakfast Muffins

These muffins are light and fluffy and make a nice treat for breakfast.

Ingredients:

3 Tbs. butter, divided
⅔ c. brown sugar, divided
2 c. flour, sifted
3 tsp. baking powder
½ tsp. salt
1 tsp. cinnamon
1 egg, beaten
1 c. milk

Directions:

1. Preheat oven to 425 degrees F.
2. Grease muffin pans and place ½ teaspoon of butter and 1 teaspoon brown sugar in each cup.
3. In large bowl, sift together, flour, baking powder, salt, and cinnamon.
4. Cut remaining butter and brown sugar into flour mixture until mixture is crumbly.
5. In small bowl, combine egg and milk.
6. Add to dry ingredients, stirring enough to moisten.
7. Fill prepared muffins pans ¾ full.
8. Bake 18 to 20 minutes.
9. Turn muffins out of tins onto a platter so that the sugary sauce runs down the sides.
10. Serve warm with butter.

Huevos Rancheros

This is a traditional Hispanic breakfast that is absolutely delicious.

Ingredients for dish:

    12 eggs, fried, cooked to taste
    12 corn tortillas, fried until crisp
    ½ c. black bean purée
        avocado roasted pepper salsa (recipe below)
        cilantro, for garnish

Ingredients for black bean purée:

    1 c. black beans
    2 strips of bacon, chopped
    ½ onion, chopped
    1 garlic clove, minced
    1 mild jalapeño, chopped
       salt and pepper, to taste

Ingredients for avocado roasted pepper salsa:

    2 avocados, chopped
    1 red pepper, roasted, diced
    1 yellow pepper, roasted, diced
    ¼ c. red onion, diced
    1 jalapeño diced
    2 Roma tomatoes, diced
    ¼ c. fresh cilantro, chopped
       juice of 1 lime
       salt and pepper, to taste

Directions for black bean purée:

1. In medium saucepan, sauté bacon until crisp.
2. Add garlic, onion, and jalapeño; cook 3 minutes.
3. Add black beans and cover with water.
4. Simmer until very soft, adding water as necessary.
5. When beans are cooked, using a hand held mixer, purée the beans until smooth.
6. Keep hot for serving or reheat when ready to use.

Directions for salsa:

1. Place red and yellow peppers in a very hot, dry skillet, or on a baking sheet under the broiler.
2. Roast until lightly blackened all around, turning as needed.
3. Immediately after roasting, place peppers in a plastic bag, and let sweat for 15 minutes.
4. Remove the skins and seeds, and chop the peppers. If you can't get all the blackened peel off, it doesn't matter, it adds to the flavor and color.
5. In large bowl, combine all salsa ingredients and adjust the seasonings.

Directions for preparation:

1. Start by spreading 1 teaspoon of warm black bean purée on each of the crisp corn tortillas, followed by the fresh avocado salsa.
2. Place the warm eggs on top and garnish with cilantro.

Sausages with Fried Apples

This recipe is a unique combination and can be served as a main dish along with fried potatoes, fresh buns, and condiments. This dish may also be used as an attractive side dish.

Ingredients:

1 lb. sausage
4 lg. tart apples, leaving skin on slice into ¼-inch pieces

Directions:

1. In large skillet, cook sausage, drain grease and keep warm.
2. Fry apple slices in sausage drippings until soft but not broken.
3. Serve sausage on hot platter, surrounded by apples.

Belgian Waffles

These waffles are hearty and delicious. We like them for breakfast, but they serve just as well as a dessert.

Ingredients for cherry sauce:

  ¼ c. sugar
  2 tsp. cornstarch
  ⅛ tsp. cinnamon
  ½ c. orange juice
  2 c. sweet cherries
  1 tsp. orange peel, grated
     sweetened whipped cream

Ingredients for waffles:

  2 c. flour
  2 Tbs. sugar
  1½ tsp. baking powder
  ½ tsp. salt
  2 c. milk
  ½ c. butter, melted
  4 eggs, separated

Directions for waffles:

1. In large bowl, combine flour, sugar, baking powder, and salt.
2. In small bowl, combine milk, butter, and egg yolks.
3. Add to dry ingredients; stir just to moisten.
4. In bowl, beat egg whites until stiff; fold into batter.
5. Bake in waffle iron.

Directions for sauce:

1. In small saucepan, combine sugar, cornstarch, and cinnamon.

2. Add orange juice, cherries, and orange peel.
3. Bring to a boil over medium-high heat; boil until thickened.
4. Serve warm sauce over waffles; top with sweetened whipped cream.

Breakfast Kabobs

Many of my family members enjoy the festive nature of kabobs, which always make an eye-catching presentation for guests.

Ingredients:

    2 c. water
    2 Tbs. lemon juice
    2 lg. Red or Golden Delicious apples
    1 lb. kielbasa or breakfast sausages
    1 bunch fresh sage (optional)

Directions:

1. Preheat oven to 400 degrees F.
2. Lightly grease a baking sheet with cooking spray.
3. In small bowl, combine water and lemon juice.
4. Core apples and cut each lengthwise into quarters, cut each quarter into 3 to 4 wedges.
5. Soak slices in lemon and water for 1 minute; drain.
6. Cut kielbasa diagonally into 24 thick, ½-inch oval slices.
7. On skewers, alternately thread 4 slices of apple and 3 slices kielbasa, beginning and ending with apple. Note: Kielbasa should be threaded through skin; not cut side.
8. Place kabobs on prepared baking sheet.
9. Roast 15 to 20 minutes, turning occasionally, or until apple slices soften and kielbasa browns.
10. Set on bed of sage leaves, if desired, and serve.

Bacon and Cheese Quiche

Our family enjoys quiche, and this is easy to make for a delightful meal.

Ingredients:

1	prepared 9-inch pie crust (see page 196)
1	c. Canadian bacon, cubed
1	sm. onion, finely chopped
¼	c. butter
4	lg. eggs
2	c. light cream or whole milk
1	tsp. salt
16	oz. mozzarella cheese, shredded

Directions:

1. Preheat oven to 450 degrees F.
2. Line pie pan with crust.
3. In large skillet, sauté onion and bacon in butter until onion is translucent and bacon warmed through.
4. In medium bowl, combine cream and eggs.
5. Beat with electric mixer until foamy.
6. Pour egg mixture into pie crust.
7. Sprinkle bacon and onion mixture on top; sprinkle with cheese.
8. Bake 10 minutes; reduce heat to 325 degrees F.
9. Bake 30 to 50 minutes more.
10. Note: When the quiche is done, the middle will have the texture of a well done omelet (spongy), and should not be watery.
11. Let sit for 15 to 20 minutes before cutting and serving.

Did You Know? . . . .

Did you know that only the U.S., Canada, Mexico, France, Australia, and the U.K. celebrate Valentine's Day?

Chocolate Chipotle Waffles

The addition of chipotle pepper powder makes these waffles unique. Try them, you'll be pleasantly surprised.

Ingredients:

    2   eggs, lightly beaten
    3   Tbs. sugar
    ¾   c. milk
    ½   tsp. vanilla extract
    ½   c. chocolate syrup
    4   Tbs. butter, melted
    1½ c. cake flour, sifted
    3   tsp. baking powder
    ½   tsp. salt
    1½ tsp. chipotle pepper powder, or to taste
         nuts, chopped
         chocolate syrup
         sweetened whipped cream

Directions:

1. In medium bowl, combine eggs, sugar, milk, and vanilla; stir thoroughly.
2. In another bowl, combine chocolate syrup and butter; cool. Stir into egg mixture.
3. In large bowl, sift together, flour, baking powder, and salt.
4. Add egg mixture to dry ingredients; stir until smooth.
5. Stir in chipotle powder, to taste.
6. Lightly grease waffle iron.
7. Heat waffle iron to medium-high.
8. Pour desired amount of batter into waffle iron.
9. Bake until indicator light goes off.
10. Lightly drizzle chocolate syrup over the waffle.
11. Top with whipped cream and nuts if desired.

Danish Pastries

Danish pastries are always an excellent choice for a leisurely breakfast or a brunch dish, and when they are homemade, they are melt-in-your-mouth delicious.

Ingredients for pastry:

3-3½ c. flour, plus 2 Tbs., divided
¼   c. water, warm
2   pkg. active dry yeast
1   c. milk
2   eggs, 1 of which has been slightly beaten
1   Tbs. sugar
1½   c. butter, cold, sliced
    powdered sugar

Ingredients for filling:

1   c. almonds or other nuts, finely chopped
½   c. sugar
1   egg
½   tsp. almond extract

Directions:

1. Measure flour onto a piece of wax paper.
2. Sprinkle yeast into ¼ cup warm water and let stand 3 to 5 minutes; stir.
3. Blend in milk, unbeaten egg, sugar, and half the flour.
4. Beat with wooden spoon until smooth.
5. Gradually stir in enough flour to make soft dough.
6. Turn out on well floured surface and let rest while making filling.
7. In medium bowl, mix all ingredients together until well blended.
8. Gently roll dough to a 14 x 10-inch rectangle.

9. Cover ⅔ of rectangle with slices of butter, leaving 1 inch of all edges uncovered.
10. Sprinkle with 2 tablespoons flour.
11. Fold uncovered ⅓ of dough over butter and press edges together.
12. Gently roll in 14 x 10-inch rectangle, having long side parallel with front edge of work surface.
13. Fold again from left and right, making 3 layers of dough.
14. Turn ¼ turn to the right.
15. Repeat rolling, folding, and turning 3 or 4 times, keeping to same size.
16. Rolling and folding makes pastry flaky; if dough becomes sticky, wrap in wax paper and chill 10 to 15 minutes between rolling and folding.
17. Roll to an 18 x 15-inch rectangle, rubbing flour on work surface and rolling pin as needed to prevent sticking.
18. Cut into 3-inch squares.
19. Put filling in centers of squares and fold corners to center, pinching points together.
20. Put on baking sheets and let rise at room temperature 1½ hours or until almost double in bulk.
21. Preheat oven to 425 degrees F.
22. Beat remaining egg and then brush tops of pastries carefully.
23. Bake 10 to 12 minutes.
24. Remove from oven; place on rack to cool.
25. Sift powdered sugar over tops.

Yields: 30 pastries.

Did You Know? . . . .

Did you know that on February 14, 1779, Captain James Cook, the great English explorer and navigator, was murdered by natives of Hawaii during his third visit to the Pacific island group?

Eggs Benedict with Hollandaise Sauce

This is an enjoyable classic and is easier to make than expected. The trick is to have everything ready and make all items at the same time.

Ingredients for hollandaise sauce:

 5 egg yolks
 5 tsp. cold water
 ¾ c. butter, softened
 ¼ tsp. salt
 1 tsp. lemon juice, or to taste

Ingredients for eggs Benedict:

 8 slices Canadian bacon
 4 English muffins, halved
 1 tsp. butter
 8 eggs
 8 truffle slices

Directions for hollandaise sauce:

1. Combine egg yolks and water in the top of a double boiler.
2. Beat with a wire whisk over hot (not boiling) water until fluffy.
3. Add a few spoonfuls of butter to the mixture.
4. Beat continually until the butter has melted and the sauce starts to thicken.
5. Care should be taken that the water in the bottom of the boiler never boils.
6. Continue adding butter, small portions at a time, stirring constantly.
7. Add salt and lemon juice.
8. For a lighter texture, beat in a tablespoon of hot water.

Directions for eggs Benedict:

1. In skillet, sauté bacon briefly in butter, and keep hot.
2. Meanwhile, poach eggs in boiling water.
3. Place each slice of bacon on a toasted English muffin half that has been lightly buttered.
4. Top each bacon slice with a poached egg.
5. Cover with hollandaise sauce.
6. If desired, garnish with a truffle slice.

Yields: 8 servings.

Bacon Cheese Puffs

This is a tasty recipe for a great brunch idea. Serve with a fruit or a green salad.

Ingredients:

1   lb. bacon, sliced
2½ c. Cheddar cheese, shredded
2   Tbs. mustard
1   c. mayonnaise
1   lb. pumpernickel bread, sliced

Directions:

1. Place bacon in large, deep skillet.
2. Cook over medium-high heat until evenly brown.
3. Drain, crumble, and set aside.
4. Preheat oven to broil.
5. In medium bowl, combine bacon, cheese, mustard, and mayonnaise; mixing well.
6. Arrange bread on baking sheet.
7. Spoon mixture onto each slice of bread.
8. Broil 5 minutes, or until bubbly.

Valentine's Breakfast Dish

This is a type of casserole that resembles a crustless quiche, and it is delicious.

Ingredients for filling:

1½ c. mushrooms, finely chopped
¼ c. green onions, sliced
1   Tbs. butter
1   Tbs. flour
¼ c. milk
    dash of pepper

Ingredients for egg mixture:

½ c. flour
2   c. milk
2   Tbs. butter
¼ tsp. salt
¼ tsp. pepper
⅛ tsp. ground nutmeg
4   eggs, slightly beaten
1   c. Cheddar cheese, shredded
½ c. red pepper, finely chopped, for garnish

Directions:

1. Preheat oven to 400 degrees F.
2. Lightly grease a 12 x 7½ x 2-inch baking dish.
3. Prepare filling first. In skillet, cook mushrooms and onions in butter until tender, 5 minutes.
4. Stir in flour and pepper to make a roux.
5. Stir in milk all at once.
6. Cook, stirring over low heat until thickened and bubbly; set aside.
7. To prepare egg mixture, in medium saucepan, whisk together flour and milk.
8. Cook and stir over medium heat until thickened.
9. Add butter, stir until melted.

10. Stir in salt, pepper, and nutmeg.
11. While continuing to stir, add eggs, combining well.
12. Stir in ¾ cup of cheese.
13. Pour half the egg mixture into prepared baking dish.
14. Spoon mushroom mixture over egg mixture.
15. Top with remaining egg mixture.
16. Bake 20 minutes, or until inserted knife in center comes out clean.
17. Sprinkle with remaining cheese.
18. Let stand 5 minutes.
19. If desired, garnish with red pepper.

Yields: 6 servings.

Finnish Soufflé

This is a light and fluffy dish that is baked in a hot oven; it will be puffy until you cut into it. This is absolutely delicious served with butter and strawberry preserves.

Ingredients:

4 lg. eggs
2 c. milk
2 Tbs. sugar
½ tsp. salt
½ c. flour
½ tsp. vanilla extract
4 Tbs. butter

Directions:

1. Preheat oven to 450 degrees F.
2. Melt butter in a 9 x 13-inch pan.
3. In medium bowl, add milk, eggs, sugar, flour, salt, and vanilla; beat well.
4. Pour batter on top of melted butter.
5. Bake 18 to 23 minutes.
6. Remove from oven; serve directly from the pan with maple syrup, jam, and butter.

Valentine's Day Omelet

*This is a nice omelet recipe to use on Valentine's Day,
as the colors will blend right in with the theme of the day.*

Ingredients:

6 lg. eggs
¼ tsp. black pepper
¾ tsp. salt, divided
⅓ c. water
1 sm. onion, diced
1 med. green bell pepper, diced
4 oz. ham, diced
8 oz. fresh mushrooms, halved
2 lg. tomatoes, each cut into wedges
4 Tbs. canola oil, divided
  parsley sprigs, for garnish

Directions:

1. In medium bowl, combine eggs, black pepper, water, and salt until well blended.
2. In a 12-inch skillet, over medium-high heat with 1 tablespoon hot cooking oil, cook onions, bell pepper and ¼ teaspoon salt until tender.
3. Add ham, and heat through; remove to small bowl and keep warm.
4. In same skillet with 1 tablespoon hot oil, cook mushrooms until golden; remove to small bowl and keep warm.
5. In same skillet, over medium heat with 2 tablespoons cooking oil, pour egg mixture into skillet; cook until set around edges.
6. With metal spatula, gently lift edge as it sets, tilting to allow uncooked portion to run under the omelet.
7. Shake skillet, occasionally to keep omelet moving freely in the pan.
8. When omelet is set but still moist, spoon ham mixture over half the omelet.

9. Tilt skillet and using spatula, fold omelet in half; slide onto heated platter.
10. Top with mushrooms.
11. Garnish platter with parsley sprigs and tomato wedges.

Potato Strawberry Crisp

This tasty cake is especially good for breakfast.

Ingredients for filling:

4 c. potatoes (4 med.), peeled, thinly sliced
2 c. fresh strawberries, sliced
¼ c. brown sugar, firmly packed
¼ c. frozen orange juice concentrate, thawed
2 Tbs. flour
1 tsp. ground cinnamon

Ingredients for topping:

1 c. old-fashioned oats, uncooked
½ c. brown sugar, firmly packed
⅓ c. butter, melted
2 Tbs. flour

Directions:

1. Preheat oven to 350 degrees F.
2. Lightly spray an 8 x 8-inch glass baking dish with nonstick cooking spray.
3. For filling, combine all ingredients in large bowl.
4. Stir until fruit and potatoes are evenly coated.
5. Spoon fruit mixture into baking dish.
6. For topping, combine all dry ingredients in medium bowl; cut in butter with pastry cutter or two knives until crumbly.
7. Sprinkle evenly over fruit and potato mixture.
8. Bake 30 to 35 minutes, or until potatoes are tender.
9. Serve warm with plain yogurt if desired.

Stuffed French Toast

This French toast is as delicious as it is filling. Serve with your favorite garnish and topping.

Ingredients:

1   loaf French bread
½   lb. breakfast sausage
½   lb. bacon
½   c. milk
4   lg. eggs, slightly beaten
¼   c. sugar
1   tsp. cinnamon
1½ tsp. vanilla extract
½   lb. ham, boiled (thinly sliced)
8   slices American cheese

Directions:

1. In a large skillet, fry bacon and breakfast sausage.
2. While meat is cooking, slice French bread into eight slices approximately 1½ to 2-inches thick.
3. Slice each slice ¾ of the way through again to form a pocket.
4. In a deep bowl, mix milk, eggs, sugar, cinnamon, and vanilla together into a batter; set aside.
5. Divide bacon, sausage, and ham into eight equal parts.
6. Dip each piece of bread into the batter, submerging so that both sides and the edges are coated.
7. Open each piece and put in one portion each of the sausage, bacon, and ham along with one slice of the cheese and close the bread again.
8. In a lightly oiled skillet, fry the stuffed, batter-coated bread slices, until golden brown on the outside and the cheese is melted on the inside.
9. Serve with your favorite garnishes and condiments.

Valentine Delights Cookbook
A Collection of Valentine Recipes
Cookbook Delights Holiday Series - Book 2

Cakes

Table of Contents

Page

Best Cheesecake

Your sweetie will be full of compliments after eating this cheesecake because it is absolutely irresistible.

Ingredients:

24 oz. ricotta cheese
2 pkg. cream cheese (8 oz. ea.)
1 c. sugar
6 lg. eggs
7 Tbs. flour
1 c. sour cream
1 tsp. vanilla extract
1 can cherry pie filling

Directions:

1. Preheat oven to 325 degrees F.
2. Wrap the outside bottom of a 10-inch springform pan with foil to prevent water from seeping in while baking.
3. In large bowl, add ricotta cheese, cream cheese, and sugar; cream until smooth.
4. Mix in eggs one at a time.
5. Add flour 1 tablespoon at a time; mix well.
6. Stir in sour cream and vanilla.
7. Pour mixture into prepared baking pan.
8. Place pan in a large rectangular pan.
9. Place the pans in the oven.
10. Add 2 inches hot water to rectangular pan.
11. Bake 1 hour 30 minutes without opening oven door.
12. Remove from oven.
13. Cool 1 hour.
14. Spread cherry pie filling over top.
15. Refrigerate until thoroughly chilled.
16. Cut into wedges.

Raspberry Bavarian Cake

This is a very refreshing pudding-style cake which is molded, then sliced after setting.

Ingredients:

1½ Tbs. unflavored gelatin
¼ c. water, cold
2 c. milk, scalded
2 eggs, separated
¾ c. sugar
1 tsp. lemon juice
1 c. fresh raspberries
½ c. heavy cream, whipped

Directions:

1. In small cup, soften gelatin in cold water, 5 minutes.
2. In small saucepan, scald milk; add gelatin mixture and stir until dissolved.
3. In top of double boiler, mix egg yolks with sugar and gradually add hot milk.
4. In double boiler, cook over boiling water for 3 minutes, or until mixture coats a spoon.
5. Remove from heat and chill.
6. While chilling, as mixture begins to thicken, add lemon juice and raspberries.
7. In medium bowl, beat egg whites until stiff.
8. Fold into raspberry mixture with whipped cream.
9. Pour all into springform pan and chill until firm.
10. Unmold and slice.

Did You Know? . . . .

Did you know approximately 1 billion Valentine's Day cards are exchanged each year?

Chocolate Cherry Cheesecake

If you like cherries and chocolate, try this cheesecake,
as it is absolutely decadent.

Ingredients for crust:

11 graham crackers
¼ c. sugar
5 Tbs. butter, unsalted, melted
    nonstick cooking spray

Ingredients for filling:

6 oz. bittersweet chocolate, coarsely chopped, divided
20 oz. cream cheese, room temperature
2 lg. eggs
1 c. sugar
2 tsp. vanilla extract
1½ c. sweet cherries, pitted

Directions:

1. Preheat oven to 350 degrees F.
2. Spray a 9-inch pie pan with cooking spray.
3. Crush graham crackers into fine crumbs.
4. Add sugar and melted butter, mixing well.
5. Press crumb crust into the pan and set aside.
6. Place a baking sheet on the center rack.
7. To prepare the filling, melt 4 ounces of the chocolate; set aside to cool slightly.
8. In a food processor, or with an electric mixer, combine cream cheese, eggs, sugar, vanilla, and chocolate, mixing until very smooth.
9. Stir in cherries, or if using a food processor, pulse a few times to mix; you don't want to chop the cherries.
10. Spoon chocolate-cherry filling into the crust.

11. Place pan on baking sheet.
12. Bake 40 minutes; the pie will be firm to touch, but still soft in the center.
13. Cool on a wire rack.
14. Melt remaining 2 ounces of chocolate; drizzle over the pie.
15. Cover loosely and refrigerate at least 4 hours, or overnight before serving.

Auvergne Cherry Cake

This is a surprisingly delicious treat, somewhat like a tart.

Ingredients:

3 eggs, beaten
4 Tbs. superfine sugar, plus extra for dusting
½ c. flour, sifted
1 tsp. yeast
1 lb. fresh cherries, stems and stones removed
   milk

Directions:

1. Preheat oven to 425 degrees F.
2. In large bowl, using a mixer, beat eggs and sugar together.
3. While continuing to mix, slowly add flour, then the yeast, mixing well.
4. Add enough milk to make a smooth, but not too thin, cake batter.
5. Butter a flan dish and pour in the batter.
6. Arrange the cherries on top.
7. Bake 30 to 45 minutes, until golden brown or inserted toothpick comes out clean.
8. Remove from oven.
9. Dust with sugar and serve either warm or cold.

Chocolate Raspberry Cake

This is an intense chocolate cake with subtle raspberry flavor, and it is made with no flour.

Ingredients:

> 12 pc. bitter (not unsweetened) or semi-sweet chocolate, chopped
> ¾ c. butter, unsalted, cut into pieces
> 6 lg. eggs, separated
> 6 Tbs. sugar
> 6 Tbs. raspberry syrup
> 2 tsp. vanilla extract

Ingredients for glaze:

> ½ c. whipping cream
> ⅓ c. dark corn syrup
> 3 Tbs. raspberry syrup
> 9 oz. bitter or semi-sweet chocolate, chopped

Directions for cake:

1. Preheat oven to 350 degrees F.
2. Butter a 9-inch springform pan.
3. Line bottom of pan with parchment paper; then butter the paper.
4. Wrap outside of pan with foil to prevent water from seeping in.
5. In heavy, medium saucepan, over low heat, stir chocolate and butter until melted and smooth (or microwave at medium, stirring frequently).
6. Remove from heat.
7. Cool to lukewarm, stirring often.
8. Using electric mixer, beat egg yolks and sugar until very thick and pale, 3 minutes.
9. Fold lukewarm chocolate mixture into yolk mixture.

10. Fold in vanilla extract.
11. In another large bowl, using clean, dry beaters, beat egg whites until stiff peaks form.
12. Gradually add 6 tablespoons raspberry syrup until all is incorporated.
13. Fold egg-white mixture into chocolate mixture in 3 additions.
14. Pour batter into prepared pan.
15. Bake 45 minutes, until top is puffed and cracked, and inserted toothpick comes out with a few moist crumbs.
16. Cool cake in pan on a wire rack.
17. Gently press down on crusty top to make cake an evenly thick cake.
18. Loosen sides of pan with small knife, and then remove pan sides.
19. Invert cake onto serving plate, and peel off parchment paper.

Directions for glaze:

1. In medium saucepan, bring cream and syrups to a simmer; remove from heat.
2. Add chocolate and whisk until melted and smooth.
3. Spread ½ cup glaze over top and sides of cake.
4. Freeze until almost set, about 3 minutes.
5. Pour additional ½ cup (or remaining glaze for a more intense chocolate flavor) over cake, smooth sides and then spread on top.
6. Chill 1 hour until glaze is firm.
7. Serve with a dollop of sweetened whipped cream.
8. Garnish with chocolate shavings.

Did You Know? . . . .

Did you know that in the middle of the seventeenth century even married people took a Valentine, and it was not always their legal other half!

Raspberry Cranberry Cheesecake

When you need a cake for a visual presentation, this is a beautiful choice. It is also delightfully flavored, with the tart cranberries and sweet raspberries, making it a mouthwatering treat.

Ingredients for crust:

1¾ c. vanilla wafers, crushed
3 Tbs. almonds, chopped
¼ c. butter, melted

Ingredients for cheesecake:

1½ c. whole, frozen, red raspberries, thawed, drained
3 pkg. cream cheese (24 oz.)
¾ c. sugar
5 tsp. cornstarch
4 lg. eggs
1 Tbs. lemon peel, finely shredded
1 tsp. vanilla extract

Ingredients for glaze:

1 c. whole, frozen, red raspberries
½ c. cranberry raspberry juice concentrate, thawed
2 tsp. lemon juice
2 tsp. cornstarch

Directions for crust:

1. Lightly grease a 9-inch springform pan.
2. In small bowl, combine crushed wafers and almonds.
3. Add melted butter; mix thoroughly.
4. Press mixture evenly in the bottom of prepared pan.

Directions for cheesecake:

1. Thaw and drain raspberries by layering paper towels on a baking sheet. Spread out raspberries.
2. Preheat oven to 350 degrees F.
3. In large bowl, with electric mixer on medium speed, combine cream cheese, sugar, and cornstarch; beat until smooth.
4. Reduce speed to low; add eggs, one at a time, beating after each addition just until incorporated.
5. Stir in lemon peel and vanilla extract; set aside.
6. Place raspberries evenly on crust, leaving a 1 inch margin around edge.
7. Pour cream cheese mixture over berries and crust.
8. Bake 15 minutes; reduce temperature to 225 degrees F.
9. Bake 1 hour and 10 minutes more, or until center no longer looks wet or shiny.
10. Turn oven off, remove cheesecake from oven and run a knife carefully around inside edge of pan.
11. Return pan to warm oven for one hour.
12. Chill. Cake may be frozen at this point.

Directions for glaze:

1. In small saucepan, combine ¼ cup concentrate, lemon juice, and raspberries.
2. Heat slowly until steam rises from top and berries are soft. Do not boil.
3. Remove from heat; strain through a fine sieve to remove seeds; return to saucepan.
4. In small cup, combine remaining ¼ cup concentrate with cornstarch, and stir until dissolved.
5. Add to raspberry mixture; cook over low heat until slightly thickened.
6. Cool to room temperature.
7. Glaze cheesecake; chill, uncovered, until serving time.

Raspberry Cream Cake

Our family loves raspberries and this is a refreshing raspberry-filled cake.

Ingredients for cake:

    4   eggs, separated
    1¼ c. flour
    ¼   tsp. salt
    1   c. sugar, divided
    2   Tbs. fresh lemon juice
    2   Tbs. water
    2   tsp. lemon peel, grated

Ingredients for filling:

    3   c. water, boiling
    2   pkg. raspberry flavored gelatin (3 oz. ea.)
    2   c. whipped cream
        sliced almonds, or pistachios, coarsely chopped

Directions for cake:

1. Preheat oven to 350 degrees F.
2. Lightly grease two 8-inch baking pans.
3. In medium bowl, sift flour with salt.
4. In large bowl, with electric mixer, beat egg whites until foamy.
5. Gradually beat in ½ cup of sugar, beating again after each addition.
6. Continue beating until soft peaks form.
7. In small bowl, with mixer on high speed, beat egg yolks until thick and lemon colored.
8. Gradually beat in remaining sugar until smooth.
9. Reduce speed to low, blend in flour mixture.
10. Add lemon juice, water, and lemon peel, beating until just combined.

11. With spatula, gently fold egg yolk mixture into egg white mixture just until blended.
12. Pour batter into prepared pans.
13. Bake 25 minutes, or until surface springs back when gently pressed with a fingertip.
14. Invert cakes onto wire rack.
15. Cool 1 hour.
16. Cut each layer in half, width-wise, to make 4 layers.

Directions for filling:

1. In small cup, stir boiling water into gelatin until dissolved.
2. Cool to lukewarm; refrigerate for 1 hour.
3. Remove from refrigerator; beat until frothy.
4. Fold into whipped cream; refrigerate until firm.
5. Spread on each layer and reassemble the cake.
6. Frost entire four layers with whipped cream.
7. Decorate with nuts.

Fudge Frosting

This was one of my mom's favorite frostings to make. Try it on your favorite cake.

Ingredients:

¼ c. butter
¼ c. milk
1 c. sugar
½ c. chocolate chips

Directions:

1. In small saucepan, combine butter, milk, and sugar; bring to boil.
2. Boil 1 minute; add chocolate chips and stir.

Ribbon of Cherry Cheesecake

This cake looks as scrumptious as it tastes. Be prepared for everyone to want seconds.

Ingredients:

- 1 c. ground almonds
- 1 c. graham cracker crumbs
- ⅓ c. butter, melted
- 2½ c. canned pie filling
- ¾ c. plus 2 Tbs. sugar, divided
- 2 Tbs. cornstarch
- ½ tsp. almond extract
- 4 c. cream cheese, softened
- 3 Tbs. amaretto flavoring
- 1 Tbs. lemon juice
- 1 tsp. vanilla extract
- 3 eggs, slightly beaten

Directions:

1. Preheat oven to 350 degrees F.
2. In medium bowl, combine almonds, graham cracker crumbs, and butter; mix well.
3. Press crumb mixture evenly over the bottom and 2 inches up the sides of a 10-inch springform pan; set aside.
4. In blender or food processor, purée cherries until smooth.
5. Pour puréed cherries into a medium saucepan.
6. In small cup, combine 2 tablespoons of sugar and cornstarch; stir into cherries.
7. Over low heat, cook, stirring constantly, until mixture is thick and bubbly.
8. Remove from heat.
9. Stir in almond extract; set aside to cool.
10. In large mixing bowl, put cream cheese, remaining ¾ cup sugar, amaretto flavoring, lemon juice, and vanilla.

11. Beat with electric mixer, on medium speed, 3 to 4 minutes, or until well mixed.
12. Add eggs all at once; beat on low just until mixed.
13. To assemble cheesecake, pour half of the cream cheese mixture into prepared crust.
14. Top with one third of the cherry purée.
15. Pour other half of cream cheese mixture onto cherry purée.
16. Top with another third of the cherry purée.
17. Using a knife or spatula, swirl cherry mixture throughout cream cheese mixture, being careful not to cut through the crust.
18. Reserve remaining cherry purée.
19. Bake 60 to 65 minutes, or until center appears nearly set when gently shaken.
20. Cool on a wire rack.
21. Refrigerate until ready to serve.
22. Cut cheesecake into wedges.
23. To serve, spoon a generous teaspoon of purée on top of each individual serving.
24. Refrigerate leftovers.

Cream Cheese Frosting

Try this delicious frosting on your special Valentine cake.

Ingredients:

    1 pkg. cream cheese, cold (8 oz.)
    5 Tbs. butter, softened
    2 tsp. vanilla extract
    2 c. powdered sugar, sifted

Directions:

1. In medium bowl, combine cream cheese, butter, and vanilla until creamy.
2. Gradually add powdered sugar, adding more if necessary until you reach the consistency and sweetness that you want.

Sweetheart Coffee Cake

This coffee cake is more like a Danish pastry ring than a cake, but either way, is still absolutely delicious.

Ingredients:

1¼ c. maraschino cherries
1 pkg. cream cheese, softened (8 oz.)
½ c. almonds, slivered
½ c. sugar
½ tsp. almond extract
2 cans refrigerated crescent roll dough (8 oz. each)
½ c. powdered sugar
1-2 tsp. milk
¼ tsp. almond extract

Directions:

1. Preheat oven to 350 degrees F.
2. Lightly grease a baking sheet.
3. Drain maraschino cherries.
4. Reserve 8 to 10 cherries for garnish; chop remaining cherries.
5. In medium bowl, combine chopped cherries, cream cheese, almonds, sugar, and almond extract; mix well.
6. For each can of crescent roll dough, press firmly at edges and perforations to make one large rectangle about 15 x 13-inches. Connect both rectangles together.
7. Spread cream cheese mixture over dough.
8. Roll up dough starting at long side of rectangle.
9. Place seam-side down on prepared baking sheet.
10. Form into a heart-shaped ring, firmly pressing ends together.
11. With scissors or a sharp knife, cut almost through ring at 1-inch intervals.
12. Turn each interval slightly on its side.
13. Bake 20 to 25 minutes, or until golden brown.

14. If necessary, cover with foil the last 5 minutes to prevent over browning.
15. Carefully remove from pan to wire rack.
16. In small bowl, combine powdered sugar, milk, and almond extract to make a glaze.
17. Drizzle over coffee cake.
18. Garnish with reserved whole cherries.
19. Refrigerate leftovers.

Sour Cream Chocolate Cake

This is another decadent cake for all the chocolate lovers out there.

Ingredients:

3 egg yolks, beaten
3 egg whites, stiffly beaten
1 c. sour cream
1½ c. sugar
1 oz. unsweetened chocolate squares
½ c. water, hot
1 tsp. vanilla extract
1¾ c. flour
½ tsp. salt
1 tsp. baking soda

Directions:

1. Preheat oven to 350 degrees F.
2. Line a 9 x 13-inch baking pan with wax paper.
3. In large bowl, beat egg yolks with sour cream.
4. Gradually add sugar and beat until thick.
5. In small saucepan, over low heat, melt chocolate and hot water. Cool.
6. Add to first mixture along with vanilla.
7. In medium bowl, sift flour, salt, and baking soda together; add to vanilla mixture.
8. Fold in egg whites.
9. Bake 45 to 50 minutes.

Sweetheart Puff

Hearts will throb when they see and taste this delightful dessert.

Ingredients:

    1 sheet frozen puff pastry, thawed
    6 oz. semi-sweet chocolate
    ¼ c. butter
    ¼ c. heavy cream
    2 tsp. vanilla extract
    1 can cherry pie filling (21 oz.)
    1 c. whipped topping

Directions:

1. Preheat oven to 400 degrees F.
2. Unfold pastry on lightly floured surface; roll out to smooth the folds.
3. Cut out a large heart shape 9 x 8-inches.
4. Put on baking sheet.
5. Wet edge of pastry with water; fold in edge toward center half an inch.
6. Press down edges with fork tines, prick center area of pastry with fork tines several times.
7. Place a piece of foil cut to fit the center of the heart.
8. Top with pie weights, dry beans, or uncooked rice to prevent puffing.
9. Bake 8 minutes; remove foil and weights.
10. Bake 4 to 7 minutes more, or until golden brown.
11. Carefully remove heart to a wire rack; cool completely.
12. In medium saucepan, over medium heat, melt chocolate, butter, and heavy cream, stirring constantly. Stir in vanilla.
13. Refrigerate 30 minutes.
14. Place heart on serving plate.
15. Spread chocolate mixture over center of heart.
16. Refrigerate another 30 minutes.
17. Spoon cherry pie filling over chocolate layer.
18. Pipe or spoon whipped topping around edge of tart.
19. Refrigerate until serving time.

Valentine Delights Cookbook
A Collection of Valentine Recipes
Cookbook Delights Holiday Series - Book 2

Candies

Table of Contents

Chocolate Covered Cherries

Try these simple, yet elegant chocolate covered cherries.

Ingredients:

20 oz. maraschino cherries with stems
12 oz. semi-sweet brown or white chocolate chips

Directions:

1. Drain cherries well; place on paper towels to finish absorbing liquid.
2. Melt chocolate according to package directions; keep warm.
3. Holding each cherry by the stem, dip one by one into melted chocolate, swirling to coat completely.
4. Place each cherry on wax paper-lined baking sheet.
5. Let stand at room temperature (or refrigerate), 30 minutes to set chocolate.
6. Store in refrigerator up to 2 days.

Yields: Approximately 4 dozen cherries.

Chocolate Kiss

This is a fun treat to make for Valentine's Day, and you can personalize it by what you write on the white paper strip sealed inside the foil wrapper.

Ingredients:

chocolate
round funnel
coffee mug
double boiler or microwave and microwave-safe bowl
nonstick cooking spray
white paper strip to write a message on
foil

Directions:

1. In double boiler or microwave, melt chocolate, watching carefully and stirring occasionally.
2. Put some tinfoil over the small end of the funnel, closing it off.
3. Spray a little nonstick spray into the funnel.
4. Place the funnel into the coffee mug to hold it upright.
5. Pour the melted chocolate in, and put into the freezer for 45 minutes to harden.
6. Take a strip of white paper and write your Valentine message on it.
7. Remove the chocolate from the funnel, and wrap it in tinfoil, tucking the message in it near the point.
8. Leave some of the white paper strip sticking out.

Cinnamon Candy

Not only do these have melt-in-your-mouth flavor and texture, they are also inexpensive to make.

Ingredients:

1 c. brown sugar, packed
2 Tbs. butter
½ c. light corn syrup
1 Tbs. ground cinnamon
½ c. water
    butter for baking dish

Directions:

1. Butter a shallow 8 x 11-inch baking dish.
2. In a medium saucepan, combine all ingredients.
3. Bring slowly to a boil and cook until candy reaches soft crack stage (275 to 280 degrees F).
4. Pour into prepared baking dish.
5. When cool, cut into squares.

Chocolate Malt Balls

When looking for a way to spend some extra time with your children, this is a fun treat to make with them. Double the recipe and you'll have plenty for a snack and a lunch box treat!

Ingredients:

    4 Tbs. butter
    2 Tbs. heavy cream
    ½ tsp. vanilla extract
    1 c. instant malted milk
    ⅓ c. sugar
    8 oz. semi-sweet or dark chocolate
        cocoa powder, for dusting

Directions:

1. In small saucepan, melt butter and cream together.
2. Remove from heat and add sugar; stir until it dissolves.
3. Cool slightly and stir in vanilla.
4. Add malted milk and stir well.
5. With your fingers, knead the mixture briefly.
6. Form into 1-inch balls.
7. Let dry for 30 minutes at room temperature.
8. Roll in cocoa.
9. Leave to dry at room temperature overnight.
10. Melt the chocolate over water in double boiler.
11. Dip the balls in chocolate to coat.
12. Store covered in refrigerator for up to 1 week.

Yields: 18 balls.

Did You Know? . . . .

Did you know that 80 percent of all Valentine cards are purchased for relatives?

Divinity

My mom used to make this divinity recipe on holidays and special occasions. She would make pink divinity with nuts for Valentine's Day.

Ingredients:

2½ c. sugar
½ c. light corn syrup
½ c. water
2 egg whites, stiffly beaten
1 tsp. vanilla extract
½ c. candied fruit or nuts, chopped
1-2 drops of red food coloring

Directions:

1. In heavy saucepan, mix sugar, corn syrup, and water.
2. Cook and stir over medium-high heat to boiling.
3. Reduce heat to medium; cook without stirring for 10 to 15 minutes, until candy reaches the hardball stage. Remove from heat.
4. With a mixer, on high speed, gradually pour hot mixture in a thin stream over stiffly beaten egg whites for 3 minutes, scraping bowl as you beat.
5. Add vanilla and, if desired, food coloring.
6. Continue beating on high just until candy starts to lose its gloss. When beaters are lifted, mixture should fall in a ribbon that mounds on itself. This final beating should take 5 to 6 minutes.
7. Immediately stir in fruits or nuts.
8. Quickly drop mixture by teaspoonfuls onto wax paper.
9. Note: If mixture flattens out, beat for another ½ to 1 minute, then continue to spoon out. If mixture is too stiff to spoon, beat in a few drops of hot water until candy is a softer consistency.

Chocolate Nut Sticks

These make a great treat for the children, and they are elegant enough to serve to company also. Dress them up even more by drizzling them with the opposite color of chocolate that you use to coat them, or add nonpareils, chopped nuts or coconut after dipping them.

Ingredients:

    2 oz. unsweetened baking chocolate squares
    ½ c. butter
    1 c. sugar
    2 lg. eggs, separated
    ¼ tsp. salt
    ½ tsp. vanilla extract
    ½ c. flour
    ½ c. pecans or walnuts, chopped
    1 pkg. semi-sweet or white chocolate chips, melted

Directions:

1. Preheat oven to 350 degrees F.
2. In microwave-safe bowl, in microwave, melt chocolate squares with butter; add 1 cup of sugar, stirring well.
3. In small bowl, beat egg whites with salt.
4. Stir yolks into the chocolate mixture, followed by the egg white mixture.
5. Stir in vanilla; add flour and nuts, mixing well.
6. Knead dough by hand, just until mixed together well; roll into finger-shaped sticks.
7. Bake 20 to 30 minutes, or until well done.
8. Cool.
9. Melt chocolate chips in a double boiler or microwave.
10. Dip cooled chocolate sticks into melted chocolate to coat.

11. Roll in your choice of decorations. Some suggestions are: coconut, chopped nuts, nonpareils, crushed toffee pieces, or any other candies of your preference.
12. Place on wax paper to dry until chocolate coating is hard.
13. Store in airtight container.

Cranberry Balls

These cranberry balls are an enjoyable candy as well as a great treat for your sweeties.

Ingredients:

12 oz. vanilla wafer cookies, crushed
1   c. powdered sugar
¼ c. butter, softened
½ c. frozen cranberry juice concentrate, thawed
½ tsp. vanilla extract
½ c. pecans, chopped
½ c. dried cranberries or dried cherries, chopped
    additional powdered sugar and/or coconut

Directions:

1. In large bowl, combine cookies and sugar; blend in butter.
2. Stir in cranberry juice concentrate; add vanilla and nuts.
3. With hands, shape the mixture into bite-size balls.
4. Roll or shake each ball in a plastic bag with the additional powdered sugar and/or coconut.
5. Arrange cranberry balls in single layer on tray.
6. Store uncovered overnight in refrigerator for best flavor.

Yields: 36 to 40 balls.

Lollipop Hearts

These lollipops are a very versatile way to tell your special someone how much you care. You can make them very simple or put extra special touches to them if you wish.

Ingredients:

8   oz. assorted red, pink, and/or clear hard candies
35-60 assorted small decorative candies, such as red cinnamon candies, small nonpareils, colored candy hearts, spice drops, gumdrops, etc.
8   lollipop sticks
8   heart-shaped cookie cutters

Directions:

1. Preheat oven to 350 degrees F.
2. Line a baking sheet with tinfoil.
3. Place unwrapped hard candies in a heavy plastic bag, then place bag between folds of a towel and break candies into small chunks with mallet or small hammer.
4. Make only 3 or 4 lollipops at a time.
5. Place 4 cookie cutters on foil, at least 2 inches apart.
6. Divide crushed candies evenly among cutters, approximately 1½ to 2 tablespoons candy per lollipop; candy layer should be ¼ to ½-inch thick.
7. Bake 6 to 8 minutes, or until candies are completely melted.
8. Remove from oven and quickly add small decorative candies to crushed candies in the cutters.
9. Cool 30 seconds.
10. Remove cookie cutters with tongs, allowing melted candy to spread slightly.
11. Quickly attach a stick to base of each lollipop, twisting the stick to cover lollipop end with melted candy.

12. If desired, press additional small candies into hot lollipops, then cool completely.
13. Peel foil from lollipops, and wrap with plastic wrap for storage at room temperature for up to 2 days.
14. These lollipops are not intended for children under the age of 3.

Yields: 8 lollipops.

Red Rock Candy

This candy reminds me of the old-fashioned fire stick candies, which every child seems to love.

Ingredients:

2 c. sugar
1 c. light corn syrup
½ c. water
½ c. red cinnamon candies
1 tsp. butter

Directions:

1. Lightly butter a 9 x 13-inch baking pan.
2. In a heavy 3-quart saucepan, combine first 3 ingredients.
3. Over low heat, cook, stirring constantly, until sugar dissolves.
4. Increase heat to medium and stir often, about 10 minutes or until mixture reaches softball stage or 234 degrees F. on a candy thermometer.
5. While cooking, add cinnamon candies and continue to stir constantly until candy reaches hard crack stage or 300 degrees F. on a candy thermometer.
6. Remove from heat; stir in butter.
7. Quickly pour into prepared pan; cool.
8. When cooled, break into small pieces.

Valentine Candy Heart

This makes a nice homemade gift for your children or your sweetie.

Ingredients:

   1¾ c. pecans; toasted, coarsely chopped, divided
   16 oz. semi-sweet chocolate
   ¼ c. butter
   12 oz. white chocolate, chopped or grated
   ¾ c. coconut, flaked

Directions:
   1. Grease an 8-inch heart-shaped baking pan; line bottom with wax paper and grease wax paper.
   2. Sprinkle 1 cup pecans evenly in pan.
   3. In top of a double boiler, combine semi-sweet chocolate and butter; bring water in the bottom of double boiler to a boil.
   4. Reduce heat to low; cook until chocolate and butter melt, stirring occasionally, and remove from heat.
   5. Wash the top of the double boiler.
   6. Place white chocolate in top of a double boiler; bring water in the bottom of double boiler to a boil.
   7. Reduce heat to low; cook until white chocolate melts, stirring occasionally, and remove from heat.
   8. Drizzle ½ cup chocolate-butter mixture over pecans.
   9. Drizzle ½ cup melted white chocolate over chocolate-butter mixture.
   10. Chill mixture in pan 15 minutes or until firm.
   11. Set aside ½ cup of chocolate-butter mixture.
   12. Combine remaining chocolate-butter mixture, remaining ¾ cup pecans, and coconut; stir well.
   13. Spread coconut mixture evenly over chilled chocolate.
   14. Chill 15 minutes, or until firm.
   15. Reheat reserved ½ cup semi-sweet chocolate mixture in top of double boiler, if necessary.
   16. Repeat for remaining white chocolate, if necessary.

17. Spoon reserved semi-sweet chocolate and reserved white chocolate by tablespoonfuls over coconut mixture, making sure chocolates do not overlap.
18. Cut through melted chocolates with a knife to create a marbled effect.
19. Cover; chill candy heart several hours or until firm.
20. Carefully invert heart; peel off wax paper.
21. Invert onto a serving plate, or wrap in decorative cellophane.
22. Serve at room temperature; cut into pieces with sharp knife.

Yields: 2 pounds candy.

Strawberry Delight Candy

These make delightful candies for a Valentine's Day treat, and they are great fun to make any other day of the year also.

Ingredients:

1 can sweetened condensed milk (14 oz.)
2 c. coconut, fine
2 tsp. almond extract
2 pkg. strawberry gelatin powder (3 oz. ea.)
    green licorice pieces
    green leaf candies

Directions:

1. In large bowl, combine condensed milk; coconut, and almond extract.
2. Add half the gelatin powder; stir until well blended.
3. Chill in refrigerator for 1 hour.
4. Roll mixture into small balls shaped like a strawberry.
5. Roll in other half of gelatin powder.
6. Top each piece of candy with a piece of green licorice for a stem and leaf candies for the leaves.

Chocolate Coffee Truffles

This recipe will turn out candies with the look and taste of a confection from a candy shop, without the expense.

Ingredients:

¾ c. whipping cream
1 Tbs. instant espresso or coffee powder
2 Tbs. coffee or amaretto flavoring
2 lb. white chocolate, finely chopped, divided
2 tsp. canola oil
3 Tbs. chocolate-covered coffee beans, finely chopped

Directions:

1. In medium saucepan, bring cream and espresso powder to a boil.
2. Pour over 1 pound of chocolate and whisk until completely melted; whisk in flavoring.
3. Refrigerate until completely chilled and firm.
4. With a teaspoon, place spoonfuls of the chocolate onto a foil-lined baking sheet.
5. Refrigerate until firm.
6. Roll into balls and refrigerate again for 30 minutes.
7. In top of double boiler, set over hot water, place the pound of chocolate and the oil.
8. Heat and stir until almost melted.
9. Remove top of double boiler from the heat.
10. Stir until chocolate has completely melted; continue to stir until chocolate has cooled and reaches a temperature of 90 degrees F.
11. Prepare two baking sheets by lining each with aluminum foil.
12. Dip each candy center in the melted chocolate, shake off the excess and place on the baking sheet.
13. When you have dipped a row of candies, top each with a little of the chopped chocolate coffee beans.
14. Before each dip, stir the melted chocolate vigorously.

15. If the centers become too soft, chill for about 30 minutes.
16. Let the candies set for 2 hours before storing in the refrigerator.
17. If the centers start to come through the bottoms of the chocolates, as often happens with soft mixtures, dip the bottoms only again in the melted and cooled chocolate.

White Peppermint Fudge

If you like peppermint, be sure to try this fudge. The cool mint is offset by the creamy chocolate, making it an irresistible combination.

Ingredients:

1½ bags of white chocolate chips or candy, chopped
1   can sweetened condensed milk (14 oz.)
1   tsp. peppermint extract
    red food coloring
    heart candy

Directions:

1. Line an 8 x 8-inch pan with foil.
2. In medium saucepan, over medium heat, melt 1 bag or 1 cup of white chocolate chips or candy with milk.
3. When mixture is smooth, remove from heat and stir for 5 minutes.
4. Add peppermint extract and stir in food coloring until desired shade of red or pink.
5. Add remaining half bag of chocolate chips or candy.
6. Stir only enough to mix in (do not allow them to melt completely).
7. Sprinkle with candy hearts.
8. Pour into prepared pan; refrigerate overnight.
9. Cut into small squares.

Easy No Beat Fudge

This is an easy-to-make fudge that is always a winner.
You may substitute the marshmallows, walnuts, and
cherries for fruit and nuts of your choice.

Ingredients:

  1⅓ c. sugar
  ⅔ c. evaporated milk
  3 Tbs. butter
  18 oz. chocolate chips
  3 c. miniature marshmallows
  ½ c. walnuts, chopped
  ½ c. candied cherries; halved

Directions:

  1. Lightly butter an 8 x 8 x 2-inch baking pan.
  2. In a heavy, medium saucepan, combine sugar, milk
     and butter.
  3. Over medium heat, heat to boiling, stirring
     constantly.
  4. Cook 6 minutes, or until candy thermometer reaches
     227 degrees F.
  5. Remove from heat.
  6. Add chocolate chips and marshmallows.
  7. Stir until melted and mixture is smooth.
  8. Quickly stir in walnuts and cherries.
  9. Pour into prepared pan and smooth.
  10. Let stand until set; cut into squares.

Yields: 3 pounds fudge.

Did You Know? . . . .

Did you know that Hallmark has over 1,330 different
cards specifically for Valentine's Day?

Valentine Delights Cookbook
A Collection of Valentine Recipes
Cookbook Delights Holiday Series - Book 2

Cookies

Table of Contents

Page

Candy Heart Cookies

These are delicious cookies to present to your family, sweetheart, or friends, and they are also a hit for a school party.

Ingredients:

½ c. butter, softened
½ c. shortening
1   c. powdered sugar
1   egg
1½ tsp. almond extract
1   tsp. vanilla extract
2½ c. flour
1   tsp. salt
½ tsp. red food coloring
½ c. peppermint candy, crushed
½ c. sugar

Directions:

1. In large bowl, cream together butter, shortening, and powdered sugar.
2. Stir in egg and extracts.
3. Work in flour and salt.
4. Divide dough in half and mix red food coloring into one half.
5. Chill overnight.
6. Preheat oven to 375 degrees F.
7. Take 1 teaspoonful of each color, roll into 3-inch long ropes, about ¼-inch in diameter.
8. Wrap 1 rope of each color around each other in candy cane pattern.
9. Place on ungreased baking sheet in the shape of a heart.
10. Bake 9 minutes, or just until done, do not brown.
11. In small bowl, combine candy and sugar.
12. Sprinkle over hot cookies.
13. Remove from baking sheet to wire rack to cool.

Gingerbread Cookies

My son loves gingerbread, and this variation of shapes makes a nice change from the traditional gingerbread men.

Ingredients:

2½ c. flour
2   tsp. cinnamon
1½ tsp. ginger
½   tsp. ground cloves
¼   tsp. salt
½   c. butter
½   c. dark brown sugar, packed
¼   c. molasses
¼   c. dark corn syrup
2   lg. eggs

Directions:

1. In large bowl, sift together flour, cinnamon, ginger, cloves, and salt.
2. In another large bowl, blend together butter and brown sugar until smooth.
3. Add molasses, corn syrup, and egg and beat well.
4. Add sifted dry ingredients, about one third at a time, mixing until smooth after each addition.
5. Chill dough 1 hour.
6. Preheat oven to 350 degrees F.
7. Lightly grease a baking sheet.
8. Roll out half of dough on lightly floured surface to ¼-inch thickness.
9. Using heart-shaped cookie cutter, press out cookie shapes or use a sharp knife to cut around a pattern.
10. Place hearts on prepared baking sheet.
11. Bake 15 to 20 minutes until golden.
12. Remove and place on wire racks to cool.
13. Decorate as desired.

Cherry Brownies

Cherries add a wonderful flavor to this iced brownie and also make an enticing presentation.

Ingredients:

- ½   c. butter
- 2   sq. unsweetened baking chocolate
- ⅔   c. flour
- ½   tsp. baking powder
- ¼   tsp. salt
- 2   lg. eggs, beaten
- 1   c. sugar
- 1½ tsp. vanilla extract
- ¾   c. maraschino cherries, well drained, halved
  extra cherries, well drained, for garnish

Ingredients for icing:

- 2   Tbs. butter, softened
- 1   c. powdered sugar
- 3   Tbs. baking cocoa
  maraschino cherry juice

Directions for brownies:

1. Preheat oven to 350 degrees F.
2. Lightly grease an 8-inch square baking pan.
3. In small saucepan, melt butter and chocolate together; set aside to cool.
4. In small bowl, mix flour, baking powder, and salt.
5. In large bowl, beat eggs; stir in sugar and vanilla.
6. Stir in chocolate mixture.
7. Add flour mixture and cherries to wet ingredients; stir to blend.
8. Pour into prepared pan.
9. Bake 35 to 40 minutes.

10. Remove from oven and cool.

Directions for icing:

1. In small bowl, blend butter, powdered sugar, and cocoa together.
2. Add just enough cherry juice until spreadable.
3. Spread on cooled brownies.
4. Cut into squares.
5. Garnish with cherry pieces if desired.

Honey Valentine Cookies

These simple butter cookies are great with the addition of almonds and honey.

Ingredients:

¾ c. butter, softened
¾ c. honey
¼ tsp. almond extract
2½ c. flour
½ c. almonds, finely chopped

Directions:

1. Preheat oven to 300 degrees F.
2. In large bowl, with electric mixer, beat together butter, honey, and almond extract until mixture is light and fluffy.
3. Add flour, 1 cup at a time, beat well after each addition; stir in almonds.
4. On an ungreased baking sheet, shape ½ cup portions of dough into heart shapes, ½-inch thick.
5. Decorate as desired.
6. Bake 25 to 30 minutes, or until edges are light brown.
7. Cool 5 minutes; remove from pan.

Hearts Filled with Love

These jelly-filled heart cookies are very flavorful and are a beautiful addition to a cookie tray.

Ingredients:

2½ c. flour
1   tsp. baking powder
½   tsp. salt
1   c. butter
1   c. sugar
1   egg, beaten well
2   Tbs. evaporated milk
1½ tsp. vanilla extract

Directions:

1. In large bowl, sift together flour, baking powder, and salt.
2. Cream together butter and sugar.
3. Stir in egg, milk, and vanilla.
4. Add flour mixture, mix well into a dough.
5. Chill overnight before using.
6. Preheat oven to 350 degrees F.
7. On a lightly floured surface, roll out dough.
8. With a heart-shaped cookie cutter, cut out an even amount of shapes as you need two for each cookie.
9. Bake 8 to 10 minutes.
10. When cooled, assemble cookies by placing a teaspoon of jelly on top of a cookie; cover with another cookie.

Did You Know? . . . .

Did you know that during medieval times, girls ate unusual foods on St. Valentine's Day to have a dream of their future husband?

Chocolate Cranberry Bars

These bars are heavenly, and they make a great lunchbox treat. Be sure to make them the night before to pack in lunchboxes.

Ingredients:

- 2 c. vanilla wafer crumbs
- ½ c. cocoa
- 3 Tbs. sugar
- ⅔ c. butter, cold, cut into pieces
- 1 can sweetened condensed milk (14 oz.)
- 1 c. peanut butter chips
- 1⅓ c. sweetened, dried, cranberries
- 1 c. walnuts, coarsely chopped

Directions:

1. Preheat oven to 350 degrees F.
2. In medium bowl, stir together wafer crumbs, cocoa, and sugar.
3. Cut in butter until crumbly.
4. In a 9 x 13 x 2-inch baking, pan, press mixture evenly on bottom and ½-inch up sides.
5. Pour condensed milk evenly over crumb mixture.
6. Sprinkle evenly with peanut butter chips and dried cranberries.
7. Sprinkle nuts on top; press down firmly.
8. Bake 25 to 30 minutes, or until lightly browned.
9. Cool completely in pan on wire rack.
10. Cover with tinfoil.
11. Let stand several hours to set.
12. Cut into bars.

Yields: 36 bars.

Chocolate Cranberry Cookies

Chocolate and cranberries make an excellent combination, and these cookies look beautiful enough to dress up any cookie tray.

Ingredients:

- 1 c. canola oil
- 1 c. sugar
- 1 tsp. vanilla extract
- 1 lg. egg
- 2 c. flour
- 1 tsp. baking powder
- ½ tsp. salt
- 2 c. fresh or frozen cranberries, coarsely chopped
- 1⅓ c. semi-sweet chocolate morsels (8 oz.)
- 1¼ c. nuts, chopped

Directions:

1. Preheat oven to 350 degrees F.
2. Lightly grease baking sheets.
3. In medium bowl, combine flour, baking powder, and salt.
4. In large bowl, cream oil and sugar until light and fluffy.
5. Add vanilla and egg; mix well.
6. Stir in cranberries.
7. Drop by rounded teaspoonfuls onto prepared baking sheets.
8. Bake 10 minutes, or until golden brown.
9. Remove from oven; let stand for 2 minutes.
10. Remove cookies to wire racks to cool completely.
11. In microwave-safe bowl, uncovered, on high power, melt chocolate for 1 minute; stir.
12. If necessary, microwave again an additional 10 to 20 second intervals, stirring, until smooth.

13. Dip half of each cookie into melted chocolate and then into nuts.
14. Place cookies on wire racks and allow chocolate to dry completely before serving or storing.

Cream Cheese Cookie Hearts

The cream cheese makes these cookies light and flaky. Use a heart-shaped cookie cutter for Valentine's Day, and change the cookie cutter to different shapes for different holidays.

Ingredients:

1 c. butter, softened
1 pkg. cream cheese, softened (8 oz.)
½ c. powdered sugar, sifted
2 c. flour
¼ tsp. salt

Directions:

1. In large bowl, cream butter and cream cheese until fluffy; gradually blend in sugar.
2. In medium bowl, stir together flour and salt.
3. Stir into creamed mixture.
4. Cover; chill dough several hours or overnight.
5. Preheat oven to 375 degrees F.
6. Divide dough into thirds.
7. On lightly floured surface, roll out dough, one section at a time. Keep the other sections refrigerated.
8. Cut out with cookie cutter to desired shapes.
9. Place on ungreased baking sheet.
10. Bake until firm, but not brown, about 12 minutes.
11. If desired, sift additional powdered sugar over slightly warm cookies.

Cupid's Cookies

The addition of oats makes this a rich and tasty whole grain cookie.

Ingredients:

1 c. butter, softened
1 c. sugar
1 lg. egg
1½ tsp. vanilla extract
2½ c. flour, sifted
½ tsp. salt
1 c. rolled oats
¼ tsp. peppermint extract
3 drops red food coloring
2 Tbs. powdered sugar
5 bars, milk chocolate, scored, broken into squares

Directions:

1. In medium bowl, cream together butter and sugar until light and fluffy.
2. Blend in egg and vanilla.
3. Sift together flour and salt.
4. Add to creamed mixture; mix well.
5. Stir in oats.
6. Divide dough in half.
7. Add peppermint extract and few drops of food coloring to half of dough.
8. Chill for several hours.
9. Preheat oven to 350 degrees F.
10. Roll out each half of dough to ⅛-inch thickness on a surface sprinkled lightly with powdered sugar.
11. Cut out one half with a 1-inch heart-shaped cookie cutter.
12. Cut out other half with a ½-inch heart-shaped cookie cutter.
13. Try to make an equal number of small and large hearts in opposing colors.

14. Place them on baking sheets.
15. Bake 10 to 12 minutes.
16. Remove from oven and immediately place one square of a chocolate bar onto the center of each large heart.
17. Place small heart on top and press lightly to secure.
18. Transfer to rack to cool.

Valentine's Day Kisses

Pecans add a delicious flavor to these chocolate kiss cookies.

Ingredients:

3 egg whites
¼ tsp. cream of tartar
¾ c. sugar
½ c. pecans or walnuts, finely chopped
¼ c. unsweetened baking cocoa
½ tsp. vanilla extract
1 pinch of salt

Directions:

1. Preheat oven to 250 degrees F.
2. Lightly grease baking sheets.
3. In medium bowl, beat egg whites with cream of tartar until soft peaks form.
4. Gradually beat in sugar until stiff, glossy peaks form.
5. Fold in pecans, cocoa, vanilla, and salt.
6. Spoon into pastry bag fitted with ½-inch tip.
7. Pipe 1-inch kisses, about 1½-inches apart, onto prepared baking sheets.
8. Bake 45 minutes, or until outside is firm but inside is slightly soft.
9. Cool on wire racks.
10. Store at room temperature, covered with plastic wrap, for up to 5 days.

Valentine Sandwich Cookies

Pink frosting makes these rich cookies very pretty.

Ingredients:

    1   c. butter
    1½ c. powdered sugar
    1   egg
    1   tsp. vanilla extract
    ½ tsp. almond extract
    2½ c. flour
    1   tsp. baking soda
    1   tsp. cream of tartar

Ingredients for frosting:

    1   c. powdered sugar, sifted
    ¼ c. butter
    ½ tsp. vanilla extract
    1   Tbs. water
    2   drops red food coloring

Directions:

1. Preheat oven to 350 degrees F.
2. In large bowl, cream butter and powdered sugar together.
3. Beat in egg, vanilla, and almond extract; mix well.
4. In medium bowl, stir together flour, baking soda, and cream of tartar; blend into the butter mixture.
5. Divide dough into thirds and shape into balls.
6. Working with one third of the dough at a time, on a lightly floured surface, roll out dough ¼-inch thick.
7. For each heart sandwich cookie, cut out 2 or 3-inch hearts.
8. Cut out the center of every other one of the hearts with the 1½-inch cutter.
9. Place each piece separately on an ungreased baking sheet, 1 to 2 inches apart.
10. Bake 7 to 8 minutes, or until light brown.

11. Cool completely on wire rack.
12. Frost bottom cookie with pink frosting and place an open centered cookie on top to form the sandwich.
13. Also frost the small, 1½-inch hearts and serve.

Directions for frosting:

1. In small bowl, combine powdered sugar and butter.
2. Add food coloring and vanilla.
3. Stir, adding water gradually until desired spreading consistency.

Secret Kiss Cookies

These cookies have a chocolate surprise in the middle and are delicious.

Ingredients:

1 c. butter
⅔ c. sugar
1 tsp. vanilla extract
2 c. flour
1 c. walnuts, finely chopped
1 pkg. chocolate kisses
powdered sugar

Directions:

1. In large bowl, with electric mixer on medium speed, combine butter, sugar, and vanilla until light and fluffy.
2. Reduce speed to low; add flour and nuts.
3. Chill dough 2 hours.
4. Preheat oven to 350 degrees F.
5. Using 1 tablespoon of dough, encase one chocolate kiss in a ball of dough completely.
6. Place on ungreased baking sheet.
7. Bake until set but not brown, about 8 to 10 minutes.
8. Remove, cool, and roll each ball in powdered sugar.

Valentine Shortbread Cookies

Adults and children alike will enjoy cutting out and decorating valentine cookies. To streamline the process, prepare the cookies beforehand – they freeze well for up to 2 weeks. Let the children ice and adorn their cookies with a variety of decorations, from sanding sugars to sugared flowers.

Ingredients for the cookies:

    1   lb. butter, softened
    1¼ c. sugar
    1   Tbs. vanilla extract
    4½ c. flour
    1   tsp. salt

Ingredients for icing:

    2   egg whites
    4   c. powdered sugar
        paste food coloring in various colors

Ingredients for the decorations:

        colored sugar crystals, sanding sugar, sprinkles
        candy dots, and/or small sugared flowers

Directions for cookies:

    1. In large bowl, combine butter and sugar.
    2. With an electric mixer, on medium-high, beat for 1 minute.
    3. Scrape down the sides of the bowl and continue beating until light and fluffy.
    4. Beat in the vanilla extract.
    5. In medium bowl, sift together flour and salt.
    6. Blend into the butter mixture, 1 cup at a time.

7. Continue mixing until the dough is smooth and no streaks of flour remain.
8. Divide the dough into four equal portions.
9. Pat each portion into a disk and wrap in plastic wrap.
10. Refrigerate for 30 minutes.
11. Working with one portion at a time (leave the others chilling), place it between 2 pieces of wax paper (or plastic wrap) and roll out ¼-inch thick.
12. Remove top piece of wax paper, and using a 3-inch biscuit or cookie cutter, cut out cookies.
13. Place cookies 1 inch apart on wax paper-lined baking sheets.
14. Reserve all of the dough scraps in a bowl.
15. Repeat with the remaining dough portions, reserving those scraps in same bowl.
16. Gather and roll the scraps; cut out more cookies.
17. Place on a second wax paper-lined baking sheet 1 inch apart.
18. Refrigerate both baking sheets until the cookies become very firm and cold, at least 2 hours or up to 2 days. (If chilling longer than 2 hours, cover loosely with plastic wrap.)
19. Preheat oven to 300 degrees F.
20. Bake the cookies until firm and golden, about 20 minutes. Do not allow them to get too dark, as they can taste slightly bitter if overly browned.
21. Cool completely on a wire rack before icing.

Directions for icing:

1. In large bowl, with an electric mixer on low speed, beat egg whites until frothy.
2. Sift the powdered sugar into the bowl. Increase mixer speed to high and continue beating until brilliant white, firm, and fluffy, about 10 minutes. This should make 2½ to 3 cups.
3. Scoop out 1 cup of icing; set aside to use for piping.

4. Thin remaining icing with water, adding 2 or 3 teaspoons at a time until it is of pouring consistency.
5. Divide the icing among as many small bowls as different shades of pink you wish to create, and then tint the portions with small amounts of coloring paste until you reach desired colors.
6. Place the cookies on a wire rack set over a baking sheet and pour the thinned icing over them.
7. If necessary, shake the cookies to ease the icing over the edges. This should cover the cookies with a thin, even layer.
8. Allow to dry completely.
9. Tint the reserved 1 cup icing, if desired.
10. Spoon into a large piping bag fitted with a number 2 plain decorating tip for squiggles, dots, scrolls, and stripes, or a number 4 or 5 plain tip, or small petal tip for piping a ribbon.
11. Pipe an icing ribbon and bow around the 1-inch cookie.
12. Pipe a series of small icing dots to resemble dotted Swiss, or pipe decorative scrolls or stripes.
13. Sprinkle the icing decorations with sanding sugar while they are still wet to make them sparkle.
14. Pipe dabs of icing and attach small sugared flowers.
15. For a paisley look, pipe or spin drops of a contrasting color of the thinned icing randomly over the surface of an iced cookie while it is still wet.
16. Using a bamboo skewer or toothpick, pull through the center of each dot.
17. For an elegant all white cookie, ice with white icing and decorate with small dots of white icing to resemble dotted Swiss.
18. Decorate iced cookies with sprinkles and/or candy dots.
19. Allow the cookies to dry for at least 2 hours.
20. If the weather is humid, dry overnight, before packaging.

Valentine Delights Cookbook
A Collection of Valentine Recipes
Cookbook Delights Holiday Series - Book 2

Desserts

Table of Contents

Page

Cherry Almond Mousse

This sweet, fruity mousse highlighted by almond flavoring is a true taste sensation for Valentine's Day.

Ingredients for mousse:

⅓ c. blanched almonds
1 c. fresh sweet cherries, pitted
¼ c. plus 3 Tbs. evaporated cane juice
1 tsp. almond extract
12 oz. extra firm silken tofu

Ingredients for topping:

1 c. fresh, sweet cherries, pitted
2 Tbs. evaporated cane juice
¼ tsp. almond extract
4 whole cherries, for garnish

Directions for mousse:

1. In food processor, process almonds to a fine powder, or into tiny granules for slightly more texture; set aside.
2. In blender, combine a heaping cup of cherries, cane juice, almond extract, and tofu, in that order.
3. Blend on low speed, stopping as needed to redistribute the ingredients, until blended.
4. Add almonds and blend to a creamy mousse.
5. Pour mixture into four long-stemmed dessert glasses; set aside, and rinse the blender.

Directions for topping:

1. In blender, combine cherries, cane juice, and almond extract; process to a thin sauce.
2. Pour over creamy cherry mousse.

3. Top with a whole cherry; chill several hours before serving.
4. Note: If blanched almonds are not available, you can easily blanch your own whole almonds by bringing 2 or 3 inches of water to a boil in a 2-quart saucepan.
5. Add whole almonds, and boil for 1 minute.
6. Drain almonds into a strainer; rub them with your fingers.
7. The loosened skins will slip right off with a little pushing motion.

Yields: 4 servings.

Cherry Fruit Dessert

If you are looking for a tasty, low fat, low calorie fruit dessert, this is really a nutritious way to go. Those who want to splurge can add a dollop of whipped cream.

Ingredients:

2 c. fresh cherries, pitted
2 med. peaches, halved, pitted
½ c. orange juice
4 orange wedges
4 cherries with stems

Directions:

1. In blender, place cherries and peaches with orange juice.
2. Blend at medium speed until creamy.
3. Pour mixture into custard glasses.
4. Top each glass with an orange wedge and a whole cherry.
5. Serve immediately.

Cherry Apple Crisp

This recipe is great during the winter months when the days are long and cold, and fresh fruit is out of season. Try this served warm with sweetened whipped cream or a scoop of vanilla ice cream on top.

Ingredients for filling:

2   c. canned sweet cherries, pitted (syrup reserved)
¾   c. cornstarch
¾   c. sugar
1½ qt. canned apples, sliced, drained
2   tsp. vanilla extract
1   Tbs. ground cinnamon
½   tsp. salt

Ingredients for topping:

4   c. old-fashioned rolled oats
2   c. flour
2   c. brown sugar, packed
1   c. butter, softened

Directions for filling:

1. Drain cherries; reserve syrup.
2. In saucepan, mix reserved syrup, cornstarch, and sugar; bring mixture to boil.
3. Stir in cherries, apples, vanilla, cinnamon, and salt.
4. Pour into a 12 x 20 x 2-inch baking pan.

Directions for topping:

1. Preheat oven to 375 degrees F.
2. In large bowl, mix oats, flour, and brown sugar together.
3. Cut in butter and mix until crumbly.

4. Sprinkle topping over fruit.
5. Bake 30 to 35 minutes, or until topping is golden brown and fruit is bubbling hot.

Fresh Cherry Streusel

This is a nice recipe for a fresh cherry streusel. You may omit the brandy if you prefer, and use a teaspoon of almond extract instead.

Ingredients:

18 oz. fresh sweet cherries, pitted
2 Tbs. sugar
2 Tbs. cornstarch
¼ tsp. ground cinnamon
1 Tbs. brandy
¼ c. orange juice

Ingredients for streusel topping:

¼ c. brown sugar
2 Tbs. flour
1½ oz. almonds, finely ground
¼ c. butter, cut into sm. pieces
   rind of 1 orange, grated

Directions:

1. Preheat oven to 350 degrees F.
2. In large bowl, combine cherries, sugar, cornstarch, cinnamon, brandy, and orange juice; let stand for 2 hours.
3. Stir; pour into a 1½-quart shallow, ovenproof dish.
4. In medium bowl, mix sugar, flour, almonds, orange rind, and butter with your fingers, until crumbly.
5. Scatter mixture over cherries.
6. Bake 30 minutes. Serve warm.

Cherry Bread Pudding

Dried cherries add a unique touch to this bread pudding. Try this delightful change to this old-fashioned dessert.

Ingredients:

    8 oz. stale, dense French bread, sliced ½-inch thick
    4 Tbs. butter, softened
    ½ c. dried cherries
    3 lg. eggs
    1 c. sugar, divided
    4 tsp. vanilla extract
    1 tsp. almond extract
    1 pinch salt
    4 c. milk, steaming hot
    ¼ tsp. cinnamon

Directions:

1. Preheat oven to 350 degrees F.
2. Butter a 1½-quart shallow baking dish.
3. Butter one side of each slice of bread.
4. Arrange one half of the bread buttered side up, in single layer in baking dish.
5. Sprinkle with dried cherries.
6. Top with another layer of buttered bread slices.
7. In small bowl, whisk eggs, ½ cup sugar, extracts, and salt.
8. Pour in hot milk in a slow stream, whisking as you pour, to make custard.
9. Pour custard over bread in baking dish.
10. Press bread into custard if it is floating.
11. Let stand 30 minutes to absorb custard, pressing again if necessary.
12. In small bowl, combine remaining sugar and cinnamon.

13. Sprinkle over pudding.
14. Place baking dish in large baking pan.
15. Pour boiling water in large pan halfway up outside of small baking dish; place in oven.
16. Bake 45 to50 minutes, or until golden on top.
17. Serve warm, topped with whipped cream.

Cherry Crisp

Serve with your favorite ice cream, or top with fresh whipped cream. Nothing could be finer than cherry crisp to serve your loved ones on Valentine's Day!

Ingredients:

½ c. sugar
3 Tbs. whole wheat flour
5 c. fresh sweet cherries, pitted
½ c. rolled oats
½ c. brown sugar
¼ c. whole wheat flour
¼ tsp. cinnamon
⅓ c. butter

Directions:

1. Preheat oven to 375 degrees F.
2. In large bowl, combine ½ cup sugar and 3 tablespoons of whole wheat flour.
3. Toss with cherries.
4. Place mixture in an 8-inch round, or 8 x 6 x 2-inch rectangular baking dish.
5. In medium bowl, combine oats, brown sugar, whole wheat flour, and cinnamon.
6. Cut in butter until the mixture is like coarse crumbs; spread over filling.
7. Bake 35 minutes, or until fruit is tender and the top turns a golden brown.

Cherry Cobbler

This is a delicious old-fashioned dessert, best served warm out of the oven.

Ingredients for cobbler:

1 tsp. butter, softened, for baking dish
1½ c. water
3 Tbs. cornstarch
1½ lb. fresh cherries, stemmed, pitted
2 tsp. lemon zest, finely grated
8 Tbs. sugar, divided
¾ tsp. almond extract
¼ tsp. nutmeg
1 Tbs. lemon juice
¾ c. flour
1¼ tsp. baking powder
¼ tsp. salt
3 Tbs. butter, softened
2 eggs
¼ c. milk

Ingredients for sweetened whipped cream:

¾ c. whipping cream
⅛ tsp. nutmeg
2 Tbs. powdered sugar
1 tsp. vanilla extract

Directions for cobbler:

1. Preheat oven to 375 degrees F.
2. Lightly butter a shallow baking dish; set aside.
3. In a 2-quart saucepan, stir together the water and cornstarch.
4. Add cherries, lemon zest, and 6 tablespoons of sugar.
5. Over medium heat, cook until mixture thickens and becomes clear, about 5 minutes.

6. Remove from heat; stir in almond extract, nutmeg, and lemon juice.
7. Transfer to prepared baking dish.
8. With an electric mixer or food processor, combine flour, 2 tablespoons of sugar, baking powder, salt, butter, eggs, and milk just until blended.
9. Drop batter by spoonfuls over the hot cherries.
10. Bake 25 minutes, or until crust is golden.
11. Cool slightly on rack.

Directions for sweetened whipped cream:

1. In small bowl, whip cream with nutmeg, powdered sugar, and vanilla until soft peaks form.
2. Spoon warm cobbler into serving bowls and top with sweetened whipped cream.

Chocolate-Dipped Strawberries

These strawberries add a festive touch to Valentine's Day.

Ingredients:

2 c. semi-sweet chocolate chips
2 Tbs. butter
  fresh strawberries with stems, rinsed, patted dry

Directions:

1. Cover a tray with wax paper.
2. In medium microwave-safe bowl, place chocolate chips and butter.
3. Microwave on high 1½ minutes or just until chips are melted and mixture is smooth when stirred; cool slightly.
4. Holding strawberry by top, dip ⅔ of each berry into chocolate mixture; shake gently to remove excess.
5. Place on prepared tray.
6. Refrigerate 30 minutes, or until coating is firm.
7. Serve within 24 hours.

Raspberry Strawberry Dessert

This recipe makes a very quick and light dessert after a meal, and is easily made ahead.

Ingredients:

    10 oz. sweetened, frozen raspberries, unthawed
    2   Tbs. orange juice
    1   Tbs. almond extract
        fresh strawberries, rinsed, hulled, halved

Directions:

1. In blender, combine raspberries, orange juice, and almond extract in blender; process until smooth.
2. If you are ready to serve, fold prepared strawberries into this mixture and serve in glasses.
3. If you make this in advance, transfer mixture to a metal bowl and freeze until ready to eat.
4. Note: If frozen solid, reprocess in blender, and then fold in the strawberries just before serving.

Raspberry Angel Dessert

Another light dessert that is simple, yet elegant to serve.

Ingredients:

    1 lg. pkg. raspberry gelatin
    2 c. water, boiling
    1 lg. pkg. frozen raspberries, thawed, drained
    1 angel food cake
    1 lg. pkg. whipped topping

Directions:

1. Dissolve gelatin in boiling water.

2. Stir in raspberries.
3. Break up angel cake and add to raspberry mixture.
4. Mix until cake is totally combined.
5. Fold in ¾ of the whipped topping.
6. Pour into mold; place in refrigerator for 4 hours until set, or overnight.
7. Before serving, remove from mold and frost with remaining whipped topping.

Raspberry Tart

Tarts are always tasty and make especially elegant desserts.

Ingredients:

1   9-inch baked pastry shell (see recipe on page 202)
¼   lb. butter, diced
¼   c. extra fine sugar
¼   c. almonds; shelled, ground
1   tsp. water
2   eggs, lightly beaten
1½ c. fresh raspberries, chilled

Directions:

1. Preheat oven to 400 degrees F.
2. In small saucepan, over low heat, barely melt butter.
3. Remove from heat.
4. Stir in sugar, almonds, water, and eggs in that order.
5. Pour chilled berries into pie shell, spreading evenly.
6. Pour almond mixture over the fruit.
7. Bake 35 to 40 minutes, or until topping is golden and puffed up.
8. Serve immediately.

Raspberry Bread Pudding

Raspberry jam adds a great flavor to bread pudding.

Ingredients:

3 c. bread cubes, toasted
4 lg. eggs, divided
4 c. milk, scalded
1 c. sugar, divided
¼ tsp. salt
1 tsp. vanilla extract
½ c. butter, melted
¾ c. raspberry jam

Directions:

1. Preheat oven to 350 degrees F.
2. Place bread cubes in a 2-quart casserole dish.
3. In small bowl, beat 2 eggs plus 2 additional egg yolks, reserving the 2 additional egg whites for the meringue.
4. Gradually beat scalded milk into the eggs.
5. Beat in ½ cup of sugar, salt, vanilla, and butter.
6. Pour milk mixture over the bread cubes.
7. Bake 25 minutes.
8. Meanwhile, in small bowl, beat egg whites until stiff, but not dry.
9. Beat in remaining sugar, one tablespoon at a time, until meringue is stiff and glossy.
10. Set aside.
11. Remove pudding from oven.
12. Spread the jam evenly over top.
13. Pile meringue over the jam, making sure to spread the meringue to edge of dish.
14. Bake another 15 minutes until meringue is set.
15. Serve.

Strawberry Raspberry Tart

This is a wonderful tart; it is very colorful and flavorful. It can be made ahead of time and stores easily.

Ingredients:

> 6 Tbs. butter, softened
> ½ c. sugar
> 1 lg. egg
> ¾ c. blanched almonds, finely ground
> 1 tsp. almond extract
> 1 Tbs. amaretto flavoring
> 1 Tbs. flour
> 2 c. fresh strawberries, rinsed, hulled
> 2 c. fresh raspberries, picked over, rinsed
> ¼ c. strawberry or raspberry jam, melted, strained
>   pastry for 11-inch tart pan (see recipe on page 202)

Directions:

1. Preheat oven to 375 degrees F.
2. Prepare pastry dough.
3. On lightly floured surface, roll pastry out ⅛-inch thick.
4. Place in an 8 x 11-inch rectangular or 10 or 11-inch round tart pan with a removable fluted rim.
5. Chill the shell while making the frangipane.
6. In small bowl, cream butter and sugar.
7. Beat in egg, almonds, almond extract, amaretto flavoring, and flour in that order.
8. Spread evenly on the bottom of the unbaked shell.
9. On middle rack, back 20 to 25 minutes, or until shell is pale golden. If the frangipane begins to turn too brown, cover the tart loosely with a piece of tinfoil.
10. Remove from oven; cool.
11. Cut strawberries, lengthwise, into ⅛-inch thick slices; arrange slices, overlapping, decoratively, alternating with raspberries in rows on the frangipane, and brush them gently with the jam.

163

Ricotta Cherry Mousse

This recipe makes a wonderful, creamy mousse that is sure to delight everyone at the table on Valentine's Day.

Ingredients:

 1 lb. whole milk ricotta cheese
 2 Tbs. honey
 1 Tbs. orange juice
 1 tsp. almond extract
 ¼ tsp. vanilla extract
 2 c. fresh cherries, pitted
 ½ c. semi-sweet chocolate shavings, for garnish
 ⅓ c. almonds, slivered, toasted, for garnish

Directions:

1. In large bowl, with an electric mixer on high speed, add cheese and whip for 5 minutes.
2. Gradually add honey.
3. Keep beating until it is well mixed.
4. Mix in orange juice and the extracts.
5. Fold in prepared cherries.
6. Divide into serving dishes.
7. Chill.
8. To serve, top with chocolate shavings and almonds.

Did You Know? . . . .

Did you know that in Wales, love spoons of wood were carved and given as gifts on February 14th? Hearts, keys, and keyholes formed the favorite theme of decorations on the spoons, which together symbolized – "You unlock my heart!"

Valentine Delights Cookbook
A Collection of Valentine Recipes
Cookbook Delights Holiday Series - Book 2

Dressings, Sauces, and Condiments

Table of Contents

Page

Cherry Sauce

This is a simple, delicious sauce to serve over your favorite cheesecake or try it on crêpes or pancakes.

Ingredients:

    1½ c. Tbs. cornstarch
    1   c. sugar
    2   c. red tart cherries, pitted
        few drops of red food coloring

Directions:

1. In medium saucepan, combine cornstarch and sugar.
2. Stir in food coloring.
3. Over medium heat, cook until thick and clear.
4. Add cherries and stir until they are warm.
5. This sauce may be served warm as a dessert topping or chilled and spread on cheesecake.

Cherry Teriyaki Sauce

This is a great sauce for marinating meat, and also to use afterward as a cooked sauce to serve alongside the meat.

Ingredients:

    3   c. teriyaki sauce
    2   c. sweet cherries, pitted, drained, liquid reserved
    1½ c. sweet cherry liquid (add water to make amount needed if necessary)
    3   tsp. ground ginger

Directions:

1. Finely chop the drained cherries.

2. In medium bowl, combine all ingredients and use as a marinade for pork, poultry, or beef.
3. Marinate meat for 1 to 6 hours.
4. After removing meat from marinade, bring marinade to boil, whisking while cooking, and serve with cooked meat or rice.
5. If desired, thicken with cornstarch by adding 4 teaspoons cornstarch to ⅓ cup of cold water, and then adding mixture to the boiling liquid in a stream while whisking.

Cherry Raspberry Sauce

This is another great sauce for serving over your favorite dessert.

Ingredients:

3 c. fresh sweet cherries, pitted
2 c. raspberries, fresh or frozen, divided
½ c. sugar
1 Tbs. lemon juice
½ tsp. almond extract
¼ tsp. ground cinnamon

Directions:

1. In medium saucepan, combine cherries, 1 cup raspberries, sugar, and lemon juice.
2. Over medium heat, stir until sugar is dissolved.
3. Bring to boil, reduce heat slightly, and cook at a low boil for 15 minutes, stirring often.
4. Transfer to a bowl; stir in remaining raspberries, almond extract, and cinnamon.
5. Cool before serving over vanilla ice cream, plain cheesecake, or angel food cake.

Strawberry Butter

This makes a great tasting butter that is great on your favorite toast, English muffin, crumpet, or bagel.

Ingredients:

- 1 pt. strawberries, or frozen, thawed, drained (10 oz.)
- ½ lb. butter, softened
- 1 c. powdered sugar (use ½ c. if using sweetened frozen berries)

Directions:

1. Place all ingredients in food processor or blender and process until smooth and creamy.
2. Chill.

Cherry Salad Dressing

The versatility of cherries is astounding. Throughout history they have been included in every sort of dish from soup to entrees to desserts. However, they are not limited to just those categories. Here, we employ fresh, sweet cherries to dress up a salad. Bursting with flavor, this exceptional salad dressing contains no oil, salt, or added sugar.

Ingredients:

- 10 oz. fresh cherries, pitted
- ⅓ c. plus 1 Tbs. raspberry vinegar
- ½ c. water
- 2 Tbs. salt-free vegetable seasoning
- 7 pitted dates, more or less, to taste

Directions:

1. Place cherries into a blender container.
2. Add remaining ingredients; blend on low speed for a few seconds.
3. Increase to high speed and blend until smooth and creamy.
4. Adjust the number of pitted dates to the sweetness of the cherries and to your taste.
5. Note: Very sweet cherries may not need any sweetening at all, while tart cherries will need more dates.

Yields: 2 cups.

Strawberry Sauce

This is a whipped cream type of sauce that is delicious served over warm pound cake, hot scones, or biscuits.

Ingredients:

5 Tbs. butter, softened
1 c. powdered sugar
⅔ c. fresh strawberries, rinsed, hulled, crushed
½ c. whipping cream

Directions:

1. In medium bowl, cream butter; slowly add sugar and blend well.
2. Gradually add strawberries, beating until smooth.
3. Add whipping cream and beat until sauce is light and barely holds a soft peak.
4. Cover and chill before using.

Strawberry Orange Sauce

This is a fresh sauce that can be used over ice cream, or cake, or even used as a dressing for salad.

Ingredients:

  1 pt. fresh strawberries, rinsed, hulled
  4 Tbs. sugar
  1 Tbs. orange juice concentrate

Directions:

  1. Crush berries or process in food processor or blender.
  2. Add sugar and orange juice, blend well.
  3. Cover and chill before using.

Maple Cherry Sauce

This is a delicious sauce, with just a hint of maple syrup flavor along with the cherry flavor. It is great served over pancake, waffles, or crêpes.

Ingredients:

  ⅓ c. cherry juice blend
  2 Tbs. cornstarch
  1 c. frozen tart or sweet cherries, thawed, drained
  ¾ c. maple-flavored syrup
  ½ c. walnuts, chopped
  1 tsp. orange peel, grated

Directions:

  1. In small saucepan, add cherry juice blend and cornstarch; mix well.
  2. Cook over medium heat until thickened.

3. Add cherries, maple-flavored syrup, walnuts, and orange peel; mix well.
4. Reduce heat to low, cook, stirring frequently until all ingredients are hot.
5. Serve warm.
6. Note: 1 can tart or sweet cherries well drained, can be substituted for frozen tart or sweet cherries.

Yields: 1½ cups.

Ranch Dressing

This is a nice low-fat version of ranch dressing, and very tasty. Use it as a dressing on your favorite salad, or as a dip with your favorite veggies.

Ingredients:

2 c. low-fat cottage cheese
½ c. low-fat yogurt, drained
2 sm. garlic cloves, minced
1 tsp. dried oregano
1 tsp. dried thyme
2 tsp. fresh parsley, chopped
½ c. buttermilk
2 Tbs. lemon juice
1 Tbs. red wine vinegar
    white pepper, freshly ground

Directions:

1. Using a blender or food processor, combine cottage cheese, yogurt, garlic, oregano, thyme, parsley, buttermilk, lemon juice, vinegar, and pepper to taste.
2. Blend until creamy and smooth.

Yields: 3½ cups.

Tart Cherry Sauce

This sauce is delightful over ice cream, cheesecake, or your favorite dessert.

Ingredients:

½ c. sugar
2 Tbs. cornstarch
1 lb. fresh tart cherries, rinsed, pitted, or frozen,
    thawed, drained
2 Tbs. butter
½ c. amaretto flavoring
    dash of salt

Directions:

1. In large saucepan, combine sugar, cornstarch, and salt.
2. Stir in cherries.
3. Cook over medium heat, stirring constantly, until sauce boils and thickens.
4. When sauce is clear and thick, remove from heat.
5. Stir in butter and amaretto flavoring.
6. Serve over ice cream, cheesecake, or your favorite dessert.

Thousand Island Dressing

This is a nice dressing for salad and even better when it is homemade.

Ingredients:

½ c. mayonnaise
2 Tbs. ketchup
1 Tbs. white vinegar
2 tsp. sugar

172

2 tsp. sweet pickle relish
1 tsp. white onion, finely minced
⅛ tsp. salt
   dash of black pepper

Directions:

1. In small bowl, combine all ingredients; stir well.
2. Place dressing in a covered container and refrigerate for several hours, stirring occasionally, so that the sugar dissolves and the flavors blend.

Double Strawberry Sauce

This is a sweet sauce that can be enjoyed over your favorite angel food cake or pound cake. Try it on your waffles, French toast, and crêpes. Enjoy!

Ingredients:

½ c. sugar
¼ c. water
3 Tbs. strawberry jam
2 Tbs. lemon juice
1 Tbs. cornstarch
1 pt. fresh strawberries, rinsed, hulled, halved

Directions:

1. In medium saucepan, combine sugar, water, and jam.
2. Over medium heat, stir until sugar is dissolved and mixture comes just to boil.
3. In small bowl, mix lemon juice with cornstarch; stir into sugar mixture.
4. Cook until slightly thickened.
5. Mix in strawberries; heat through but do not cook.
6. Also can be served over frozen yogurt or pudding.

Strawberry Vinegar

Make your own strawberry vinegar for use on fruits, salads, or in vinaigrette.

Ingredients:

> 1 pt. strawberries, hulled, sliced
> 2 c. white wine vinegar
> 2 Tbs. sugar

Directions:

1. In medium bowl, stir together strawberries, vinegar, and sugar.
2. Let stand, covered, at room temperature for 2 days.
3. Note: This vinegar will keep in a dark, cool place indefinitely.

Strawberry Vinaigrette

This is a perfect dressing to pour over a spinach salad with fresh strawberries, toasted almonds, and blue cheese.

Ingredients:

> 1 c. olive oil
> ½ pt. fresh strawberries, halved
> 2 Tbs. balsamic vinegar
> ½ tsp. salt
> ¼ tsp. ground black pepper
> ¼ tsp. dried tarragon
> ¼ tsp. sugar

Directions:

1. In blender or food processor, combine all ingredients; blend until smooth.

Valentine Delights Cookbook
A Collection of Valentine Recipes
Cookbook Delights Holiday Series - Book 2

Jams, Jellies, and Syrups

Table of Contents

Page

A Basic Guide for Canning Jams, Jellies, and Syrups

1. Wash jars in hot, soapy water inside and out with brush or soft cloth.
2. Run your finger around rim of each jar, discarding any with cracks or chips.
3. Rinse well in clean, clear, hot water, using tongs to avoid burns to hands or fingers.
4. Place upside down on clean cloth to drain well.
5. Place lids in boiling water for 2 minutes to sterilize and keep hot until placing on rim of jar.
6. Immediately prior to filling each jar with hot food, immerse in hot water for 1 minute to heat jars. Heating jars avoids breakage.
7. Fill each jar to within ⅛ inch of top of rim or to level recommended in recipe.
8. Wipe rims of jars with clean, damp cloth to remove any particles of food, and check again for any chips or cracks.
9. Using tongs, place lids from hot bath directly onto jars.
10. Place rings over lids, and using cloth, gloves, or holders, tighten down firmly while hanging onto jars.
11. Do not tighten lids down too hard as air may become trapped in jars and prevent them from sealing.
12. Place on protected surface to cool, taking care to not disturb lid and ring. Lids will show slight indentation when sealed.
13. Leave overnight until thoroughly cooled.
14. When cooled, wipe jars with damp cloth, and then label and date each.
15. Store upright on shelf in cool, dark place.

Strawberry Jam

What cookbook would be complete without the traditional strawberry jam recipe?

Ingredients:

    2 lb. fresh strawberries, rinsed, hulled
    4 c. sugar
    ¼ c. lemon juice

Directions:

1. In large bowl, crush strawberries in batches until you have 4 cups of mashed berries.
2. In a heavy saucepan, mix together the strawberries, sugar, and lemon juice.
3. Over low heat, stir until sugar is dissolved.
4. Increase heat to high; bring mixture to a full rolling boil. Boil until mixture reaches 220 degrees F.
5. Process by testing for jelling first. To test for jelling, place three plates in a freezer.
6. After 10 minutes of boiling the jam at 220 degrees F., place a teaspoon of the liquid onto one of the cold plates from the freezer.
7. Return the plate with the liquid to the freezer for a minute; run your finger through the jam on the plate. If it doesn't try to run back together (if you can make a line through it with your finger), it's ready to be canned.
8. Process following A Basic Guide for Canning on page 176.

Did You Know? . . . .

Did you know that 73 percent of people who buy flowers for Valentine's Day are men?

Apple Raspberry Jelly

This jelly is absolutely delicious and is a different combination than is usually found. This recipe may be canned or frozen to keep over winter.

Ingredients:

 1   c. red raspberry juice
 2   c. apple juice
 5¼ c. sugar
 1   pkg. pectin
 ½   tsp. butter

Directions:

1. Pour juices into a 6 to 8-quart kettle.
2. In separate bowl, measure sugar.
3. Add pectin and butter to juices.
4. Over high heat, bring mixture to full rolling boil, stirring constantly.
5. Quickly stir sugar into juices and bring mixture back to full rolling boil.
6. Boil for 1 minute, stirring constantly.
7. Mixture will rise to within 2 inches of the top of the pan, so make sure you stir continuously.
8. Remove from heat and skim foam with spoon.
9. Process following A Basic Guide for Canning on page 176.

Cherry Raspberry Jam

This is a delicious jam, and it is good on everything from toast to biscuits.

Ingredients:

 1   qt. fresh sweet cherries, pitted, chopped

¼ c. orange juice
2   Tbs. lemon rind
1   Tbs. orange peel, grated
1½ qt. raspberries
1   qt. sugar

Directions:

1. In large saucepan, add cherries, orange juice, lemon rind, and orange peel.
2. Bring to boil; cook 10 minutes, stirring frequently.
3. Stir in raspberries and sugar; return to boil, stirring frequently.
4. Boil 15 minutes, or to jam stage.
5. Remove from heat. Stir and skim for 5 minutes.
6. Process following A Basic Guide for Canning on page 176.

Fresh Strawberry Syrup

This syrup is delicious on pancakes, waffles, French toast, bagels, or anything else you want to put it on.

Ingredients:

1 qt. fresh strawberries, sliced
½ c. sugar
¼ c. orange liqueur or orange juice
1 tsp. orange rind, grated

Directions:

1. In medium saucepan, combine all ingredients.
2. Let stand 30 minutes, or until sugar dissolves.
3. Cook over low heat, stirring occasionally, 5 minutes or until warm.

Yields: 2 cups.

Quick Raspberry Jelly

This jelly is quick to make because it uses already prepared juice, but it is still delicious, and you will get you out of the kitchen in a jiffy.

Ingredients:

    20 oz. raspberry juice
    ¾ c. water
    2 c. sugar
    6 oz. liquid pectin
    5 jars (½ pt. is best)

Directions:

1. In heavy, large saucepan, combine raspberry juice, water, and sugar.
2. Over high heat, bring to boil stirring constantly.
3. Stir in pectin and quickly bring to a full rolling boil (liquid will continue to boil when stirred); boil 1 minute.
4. Remove from heat, skim off foam.
5. Process following A Basic Guide for Canning on page 176.

Freezer Raspberry Jam

Making freezer jam helps to keep the color bright and the taste as fresh as if the fruit was picked this morning.

Ingredients:

    2 c. raspberries, finely crushed
    3 c. sugar
    1 pkg. powdered fruit pectin
    1 c. water

Directions:

1. In large bowl, combine fruit and sugar.
2. Let stand for 20 minutes, stirring occasionally.
3. In large saucepan, boil pectin and water rapidly for 1 minute, stirring constantly.
4. Remove from heat.
5. Add raspberries and stir about 2 minutes.
6. Pour into containers and cover.
7. Let stand at room temperature for 1 hour.
8. Refrigerate until set.
9. Store in freezer.
10. Once opened, refrigerate.

Rhubarb Strawberry Jam

This is a traditional way to make rhubarb jam, and the strawberry gelatin really does add quite a bit of flavor to the recipe.

Ingredients:

5 c. fresh rhubarb, chopped
3 c. sugar
1 pkg. strawberry flavored gelatin (3 oz.)

Directions:

1. In large saucepan or stockpot, combine rhubarb and sugar; cover and let stand overnight.
2. Over medium heat, bring rhubarb and sugar to a boil.
3. Reduce heat to low; boil, stirring constantly for 12 minutes.
4. Remove from heat and stir in dry gelatin mix.
5. Process following A Basic Guide for Canning on page 176.

Freezer Strawberry Jam

This is an easy-to-make strawberry jam which retains its fresh-picked taste and bright color because the fruit isn't cooked.

Ingredients:

2 c. strawberries, finely crushed
3 c. sugar
1 pkg. powdered fruit pectin
1 c. water

Directions:

1. In large bowl, combine fruit and sugar; let stand 20 minutes, stirring occasionally.
2. In large saucepan, boil pectin and water rapidly for 1 minute, stirring constantly.
3. Remove from heat.
4. Add strawberries and stir for 2 minutes.
5. Pour into containers and cover.
6. Let stand at room temperature for 1 hour.
7. Refrigerate until set.
8. Store in freezer.
9. Once opened, refrigerate.

No Cook Apple Raspberry Jam

There is nothing like the great, flavorful combination of apples and raspberries. This hearty, no cook jam is tasty and delicious on warm toast with butter.

Ingredients:

3 c. fully ripe raspberries
1 c. apples, peeled, cored, finely ground
4 c. sugar
2 Tbs. fresh lemon juice
1 pouch liquid fruit pectin

Directions:

1. Thoroughly crush berries using a blender, sieve half of pulp to remove some seeds, if desired.
2. Measure 1½ cups prepared berries; pour into large bowl. Add apples.
3. Add sugar to bowl; mix well; let stand 10 minutes.
4. Add lemon juice and pectin to bowl; stir 3 minutes.
5. Ladle jam into clean containers, leaving ¼-inch headspace. Cover with tight fitting lids.
6. Let stand at room temperature until set.
7. Store in freezer.
8. Jam can be stored in the refrigerator if used within 3 weeks.

Cherry Conserve

These conserves are delicious when served with toast, and it is wonderful on pancakes or waffles.

Ingredients:

5 lb. Bing cherries, washed, pitted
1 orange, seeded, thinly sliced
4 c. sugar
1 c. almonds or pecans, chopped
1 c. seedless raisins
  juice of 1 lemon

Directions:

1. In a preserving kettle, put cherries, orange slices, lemon juice, and sugar; mix well.
2. Over low-medium heat, cook mixture, uncovered, 45 minutes, stirring frequently until thick and transparent; remove from heat.
3. Skim off the foam with a metal spoon.
4. Add nuts and raisins; cook 10 minutes.
5. Process following A Basic Guide for Canning on page 176.

Rhubarb Cherry Jelly

This is an easy to make version of jelly because of the gelatin and the pie filling, but nonetheless, it is delicious.

Ingredients:

6 c. rhubarb, diced
4 c. sugar
1 can cherry pie filling (21 oz.)
1 lg. pkg. cherry flavored gelatin (6 oz.)

Directions:

1. Place rhubarb in a large bowl.
2. Pour sugar over top and stir to coat.
3. Cover bowl and refrigerate overnight.
4. Place rhubarb mixture in a large saucepan; over medium heat, cook until tender, stirring frequently.
5. Stir in pie filling and gelatin; bring mixture to boil.
6. Pour into a shallow pan and cool in refrigerator.
7. Pack into jars or plastic containers.
8. Must be refrigerated or frozen.

Triple Berry Jam

This jam is the ultimate of jams, with the 3 different berries in it. Try it on buttered toast or biscuits, or fresh bread, right out of the oven. Yum!

Ingredients:

4 c. fresh or frozen strawberries, thawed
2 c. fresh or frozen raspberries, thawed
1 c. fresh or frozen blueberries, thawed
1 pkg. pectin (1¾ oz.)

Directions:

1. Mash strawberries, raspberries, and blueberries by hand or with food processor to make 4 cups pulp.

2. Stir in pectin; let stand 10 minutes, stirring frequently.
3. Transfer to large saucepan.
4. Over medium heat, cook and stir until mixture comes to a boil.
5. Cook and stir 1 minute more.
6. Remove from heat; skim off foam if necessary.
7. Immediately fill containers, leaving ½-inch headspace. Place lids on containers.
8. Let stand at room temperature until firm.
9. Store up to 2 weeks in refrigerator or 3 months in freezer.

Raspberry Jalapeño Jelly

This jelly is very good when served over pork or used as a glaze on grilled chicken.

Ingredients:

1 c. fresh or frozen raspberries
½ c. green bell pepper, chopped
¼ c. jalapeño pepper, chopped
3 c. white sugar
¾ c. apple cider vinegar
6 fl. oz. liquid pectin
1 sprig fresh mint

Directions:

1. In saucepan, combine raspberries, bell pepper, and jalapeño peppers with sugar and cider vinegar.
2. Over medium-high heat, bring to boil; boil rapidly for 1 minute.
3. Remove from heat and let stand for 5 minutes.
4. Stir in pectin; run mixture through a strainer to remove bits of peppers and skins.
5. Process following A Basic Guide for Canning on page 176.
6. Refrigerate after opening.

Cherry Jam

Some people find that cherry jam can be hard to make because of the low acid and pectin in cherries, but don't be discouraged. This jam is delicious and well worth the effort.

Ingredients:

    10 lb. cherries, pitted, with the pits preserved
    5 lemons, juiced
    14 c. sugar

Directions:

1. In large preserving kettle, put cherries and lemon juice.
2. Put cherry pits in a cheesecloth bag and add to the pan.
3. Over low-medium heat, bring to a boil.
4. Simmer 30 minutes, or until the cherries are tender.
5. Remove the bag of pits.
6. Reduce heat to low.
7. Add sugar and stir until it has dissolved.
8. Increase heat to medium.
9. Bring to a boil and cook briskly until the mixture sets.
10. With a slotted spoon, dipped in boiling water and dried, quickly remove the scum from the surface of the jam.
11. Allow the jam to cook in the pan until a thin skin forms on the surface.
12. Process following A Basic Guide for Canning on page 176.

Did You Know? . . . .

Did you know that Valentine's Day was originally associated with the mating season of birds?

Valentine Delights Cookbook

A Collection of Valentine Recipes
Cookbook Delights Holiday Series - Book 2

Main Dishes

Table of Contents

Page

Salmon in Tomato Sauce

This is a nicely flavored dish that is not too heavy, and it makes a great dish for a special occasion.

Ingredients:

6   oz. smoked salmon, thinly sliced
8   oz. angel hair pasta
1   lg. garlic clove, minced
3   Tbs. olive oil
2¼ c. tomatoes, seeded, chopped, divided
½   c. dry white wine
3   Tbs. large capers, drained
1½ tsp. dill weed
1½ tsp. sweet basil
½   c. Parmesan cheese, freshly grated
     parsley, for garnish

Directions:

1. Cut smoked salmon with the grain, into ½-inch wide strips; reserve.
2. Cook pasta according to package directions.
3. In large skillet, over medium-high heat, heat oil until hot.
4. Add garlic; stir and cook until a golden color.
5. Add 2 cups of tomatoes, wine, capers, dill weed, and basil.
6. Stir and cook until mixture is hot.
7. Drain pasta,
8. Place in a large serving bowl.
9. Toss angel hair with tomato mixture.
10. Add smoked salmon and cheese; toss gently.
11. Garnish with remaining tomatoes and parsley, if desired.
12. Serve immediately.

Cherry Almond Glazed Pork

This is a nice glaze for a pork roast, adding flavor and color. Serve some sauce on the side also, and everyone will be sure to comment.

Ingredients:

- 3 lb. pork loin roast
- 1 jar cherry preserves (12 oz.)
- 2 Tbs. light corn syrup
- 2 Tbs. vinegar
- ¼ tsp. salt
- ¼ tsp. ground cinnamon
- ¼ tsp. ground nutmeg
- ¼ tsp. ground cloves
- 3 Tbs. slivered almonds, toasted
  salt and pepper, to taste

Directions:

1. Preheat oven to 325 degrees F.
2. Rub the roast with a little salt and pepper.
3. Place it on a rack, in a shallow baking pan.
4. Roast uncovered for 2 to 2½ hours.
5. In medium saucepan, combine cherry preserves, corn syrup, vinegar, salt, cinnamon, nutmeg, and cloves.
6. Heat to boiling, stirring frequently.
7. Reduce heat and simmer 2 minutes more.
8. Stir in toasted almonds; keep the sauce warm until ready to serve.
9. When meat is done, spoon enough hot cherry sauce over the roast to glaze.
10. Return to oven for 30 minutes more, or until meat thermometer reads 170 degrees F.
11. Baste roast with sauce several times during last 30 minutes.

Salmon in Coconut Milk

This is a traditional Hispanic dish, and it is absolutely mouth watering. I suggest serving it with Hispanic rice and a simple salad to complement the awesome flavor of the fish.

Ingredients:

4   thick salmon steaks
1   pc gingerroot, peeled, thin slices (1-inch piece)
2   lg. garlic cloves, peeled, thin slices
12 oz. tomatoes, peeled, chopped
1   fresh red chili pepper, seeded, thinly sliced
1   yellow bell pepper, seeded, chopped
4-6 cardamom pods, roughly crushed
1   can coconut milk (14 oz.)
2   limes, juice only
    handful of fresh mint leaves, chopped
    sea salt, to taste

Directions:

1. Preheat oven to 300 degrees F.
2. Put fish steaks in a shallow ovenproof dish with a lid, into which they fit quite closely.
3. Scatter the ginger, garlic, tomato, chili and yellow pepper over and around the fish and place the cardamom pods in between.
4. Empty coconut milk into a separate bowl, add a good sprinkling of sea salt and gradually stir in the lime juice.
5. Pour mixture gently over and around the fish and cover the dish.
6. Place dish on center rack.
7. Cook 40 to 50 minutes, or until the fish is lightly done. To test, insert a small, sharp knife into the

center of one of the steaks. If the flesh is slightly darker pink in the center it will be perfectly cooked.
8. Remove from oven.
9. Before serving, scatter mint leaves on top.

Baked Ham with Cherry Glaze

A fruity red glaze is a wonderful addition to your baked ham, making it look festive and delicious.

Ingredients:

2   c. canned cherries, juice reserved
¾   c. juice from cherries
1½ Tbs. cornstarch
¾   c. apple juice
2   Tbs. vinegar
2   Tbs. liquid glucose
2   Tbs. lemon juice
2-4 lb. ham, canned
    several drops of red food coloring

Directions:

1. Preheat oven to 350 degrees F.
2. Drain and pit cherries.
3. In small saucepan, add cherry juice and cornstarch; stir until smooth.
4. Add apple juice, vinegar, and liquid glucose.
5. Over medium heat, bring to boil stirring constantly.
6. Stir in lemon juice, red food coloring, and cherries.
7. Cut ham into slices.
8. Place in shallow roasting pan and tie with string to hold in shape.
9. Glaze ham with cherry sauce.
10. Bake 30 minutes for 2-pound ham, or 45 to 60 minutes for 4-pound ham.

Chicken Pepperoni

This is a wonderfully flavored Italian dish that the whole family enjoys. We serve it over a bed of pasta noodles, along with a green salad and crusty French bread to make the meal complete.

Ingredients:

½ lb. of your favorite pasta
3 oz. pepperoni, diced
⅓ c. flour
½ tsp. salt
¼ tsp. freshly ground pepper
½ tsp. ground oregano
½ tsp. basil, crushed
½ tsp. garlic powder
½ tsp. onion powder
1 lb. boneless skinless chicken breast
1 can tomato sauce (16 oz.)
1 can tomato paste (6 oz.)
½ tsp. red pepper flakes, or more to taste, crushed
½ c. water
   olive oil, if necessary

Directions:

1. Cook pasta according to package directions.
2. Dice pepperoni into ¼-inch cubes and cook in a skillet over medium heat, allowing the fat to render out.
3. Remove from pan and set aside.
4. In small bowl, combine flour with salt, pepper, oregano, basil, garlic powder, and onion powder.
5. Cut chicken into bite-size chunks.
6. Dredge chicken pieces in seasoned flour until coated.

7. Shake off excess flour and brown in the rendered pepperoni fat (and olive oil, if needed) until the chicken is almost cooked.
8. Remove from pan and set aside.
9. In frying pan, whisk together the tomato sauce, tomato paste, red pepper flakes and ½ cup of water until smooth.
10. Return chicken and pepperoni to pan.
11. Bring to simmer; cook, stirring, for 5 to 7 minutes.
12. Serve over a bed of pasta.

Apple Turkey Rolls

This tasty turkey roll can be served to company as an appetizer or as a main dish.

Ingredients:

1 lb. ground turkey
2 c. apples, diced
2 c. bread crumbs
1 sm. onion, diced
½ tsp. sage
½ tsp. poultry seasoning
½ c. Cheddar cheese, grated

Directions:

1. Preheat oven to 350 degrees F.
2. On wax paper, roll turkey into a rectangle ½-inch thick.
3. In medium bowl, combine apples, bread crumbs, and onions; spread over meat.
4. Start from the long end and roll as for jellyroll.
5. Place in a 9 x 13-inch baking dish.
6. Bake 35 minutes; sprinkle grated cheese over top of roll and bake 10 more minutes.
7. Slice and serve on a serving platter.

Chicken Rolls with Filling

This dish is a wonderful change of pace from your simple chicken dish. Serve side dishes of chicken gravy, mashed potatoes, and your choice of veggies to complete the meal.

Ingredients:

4 chicken breast halves, skinless boneless, flattened
⅓ c. orange juice
⅔ c. plus 2 Tbs. dried cranberries, divided
5 Tbs. butter, divided
¼ c. celery, chopped
¼ c. green onion, chopped
1 c. herb stuffing mix, crushed, divided
½ tsp. ground sage
½ tsp. white pepper
3 Tbs. honey mustard
   cooking spray
   tomato rosettes
   parsley sprigs, for garnish

Directions:

1. Preheat oven to 350 degrees F.
2. Line a baking sheet with tinfoil and lightly spray with cooking spray.
3. In small saucepan, over medium heat, heat orange juice.
4. Add cranberries; cover and set aside to soften.
5. In another saucepan, over medium heat, melt 2 tablespoons of the butter.
6. Add celery and onion; sauté for 2 minutes.
7. To ⅓ cup of the stuffing mix, add sage.
8. Stir into celery mixture.
9. Add ⅔ cup of the moistened cranberries.
10. Sprinkle chicken with pepper.
11. Spread with honey mustard.
12. Spoon cranberry mixture in center of each piece of chicken.

13. Roll chicken over filling; fasten with wooden toothpicks.
14. In small saucepan, melt remaining 3 tablespoons of butter; dip each chicken roll, first in butter and then in remaining ⅔ cup crushed stuffing.
15. Place chicken on prepared baking pan.
16. Bake, uncovered for 30 minutes, or until fork can be inserted in chicken with ease.
17. Garnish with tomato rosettes and parsley sprigs.
18. Sprinkle chicken with remaining 2 tablespoons cranberries before serving.

Chicken Parmesan

This is a traditional chicken Parmesan recipe that is a favorite in our family, and it is so easy to make that we make it often on busy nights in our household.

Ingredients:

4   boneless skinless chicken breast halves
1   egg, slightly beaten
½   c. seasoned bread crumbs
2   Tbs. butter
1¾ c. spaghetti sauce
½   c. mozzarella cheese, shredded
1   Tbs. Parmesan cheese, grated
¼   c. fresh parsley, chopped

Directions:

1. Using bottom of small bottle, lightly pound chicken and flatten to even thickness.
2. Dip chicken into egg, then into crumbs to coat.
3. In skillet over medium heat, in hot butter, brown chicken on both sides; add sauce.
4. Reduce heat; cover and simmer for 10 minutes.
5. Sprinkle with cheeses and parsley.
6. Cover; simmer 5 minutes, or until cheese melts.

Yields: 4 servings.

Spaghetti with Meatballs

This recipe has traditional meatballs, and the children especially seem to like them.

Ingredients for sauce:

2   Tbs. olive oil
1½ c. onion, chopped
2   garlic cloves, minced
2   cans tomatoes, diced with juice (28 oz. each)
4   Tbs. fresh basil, chopped
    salt and pepper, to taste

Ingredients for meatballs:

⅔   c. bread crumbs, fresh
3   Tbs. milk
⅓   c. Parmesan cheese, freshly grated
¼   c. onion, finely chopped
1   lg. egg
1   garlic clove, minced
¼   Tbs. black pepper, ground
1   lb. sweet Italian sausages, casings removed
1   lb. spaghetti pasta

Directions for sauce

1. In large saucepan, over medium heat, heat oil.
2. Add onion; sauté until golden, about 10 minutes.
3. Add garlic; stir 1 minute.
4. Add tomatoes with juices, 2 tablespoons basil; salt and pepper, to taste; bring to boil.
5. Reduce heat; simmer 1 hour, until sauce thickens, breaking up tomatoes with fork; set aside.

Directions for meatballs:

1. Preheat oven to 350 degrees F.
2. Lightly grease a baking sheet.
3. In medium bowl, mix crumbs and milk; let stand 5 minutes.

4. Mix in Parmesan, onion, remaining basil, egg, garlic, and pepper.
5. Add sausage and blend well.
6. Using wet hands, form mixture into 1¼-inch balls.
7. Place on prepared baking sheet.
8. Bake 30 minutes, until meatballs are light brown and cooked through; add to sauce.
9. In large saucepan, in salted water, cook pasta until jut tender, but still firm to bite; drain.
10. Bring sauce and meatballs to simmer.
11. Spoon over spaghetti, and serve.

Cherry Yogurt Chicken

This recipe is written for a crowd and is a nicely flavored dish that is relatively simple to prepare.

Ingredients:

12 boneless skinless chicken breast halves (5 oz. ea.)
1   c. Italian dressing
3   oz. green onions, sliced
1   tsp. canola oil
¾   c. maraschino cherries, drained, finely chopped
2   c. maraschino cherry juice
¾   c. lemon juice
¾   c. vanilla or plain yogurt

Directions:

1. In covered container, marinate chicken breasts in Italian dressing at least two hours, or overnight in refrigerator.
2. In frying pan, heat oil; sauté green onions and drain.
3. Add maraschino cherry juice and lemon juice.
4. Simmer until reduced by half.
5. Stir in vanilla yogurt to thicken slightly.
6. Keep warm until serving.
7. Remove chicken from marinade; drain well.
8. Grill or bake chicken breasts until done.
9. Spoon ¼ cup of sauce over chicken and serve.

Heart-Shaped Pizza

These make colorful, romantic pizzas that taste good.

Ingredients:

  1 can refrigerated pizza crust dough (10 oz.)
  4 tsp. butter, divided
  ½ med. red pepper, thinly sliced
  1 lg. leek, cut into 1-inch strips
  1 boneless skinless chicken breast half, cubed
  ¼ c. pesto, refrigerated
  3 canned artichoke hearts, coarsely chopped
  4 oz. fontina cheese, shredded
  ½ c. mozzarella cheese, shredded
  ½ tsp. dried oregano

Directions:

  1. Preheat oven to 425 degrees F.
  2. Lightly grease a baking sheet.
  3. Unroll pizza dough into a rectangle or square shape.
  4. Create a heart-shaped template out of paper towels.
  5. Place template on dough and cut around heart shape using scissors.
  6. Place heart-shaped dough on prepared baking sheet.
  7. Bake following package directions for prebaking pizza crust; set aside.
  8. In skillet, sauté red pepper and leeks in half of the butter until almost tender; remove from skillet.
  9. Add chicken and other half of the butter to skillet.
  10. Cook until chicken is done and lightly browned.
  11. Spread pesto over prebaked pizza crust.
  12. Top with sautéed leeks, red peppers, and chicken.
  13. Add artichoke hearts.
  14. Top with cheeses, and sprinkle with oregano.
  15. Bake 7 to 10 minutes.
  16. Note: With portion of dough that has been cut away, slice in strips, bake, and serve with dipping sauce or garlic Parmesan butter.

Creamy Salmon Lasagna

This dish is very creamy and delicious. Using canned salmon is an economical and tasty way to get more vitamins and minerals into your family's diet.

Ingredients:

½   c. butter
½   c. flour
3½ c. milk
1⅛ oz. ricotta cheese
¼   c. frozen spinach, thawed, well drained
¾   c. extra milk
1   can red salmon, drained, flaked (15 oz.)
2   ripe tomatoes, diced
1   pkg. fresh lasagna sheets (14 oz.)
¾   c. Parmesan cheese, grated

Directions:

1. Preheat oven to 350 degrees F.
2. In small saucepan, melt butter.
3. Remove from heat; add flour and stir until smooth.
4. Gradually add milk, stirring well to remove lumps.
5. Return to heat; stir constantly until boiling.
6. Remove from heat.
7. In small bowl, mix ricotta with spinach and extra milk; season with salt and pepper.
8. In another small bowl, mix salmon and tomatoes.
9. Using a 9 x 13-inch ovenproof dish, layer the ingredients as follows: lasagna sheets; white sauce; lasagna; ricotta mixture; lasagna; salmon mixture.
10. Repeat layers to use up all mixtures ending with white sauce.
11. Sprinkle with Parmesan.
12. Bake 40 to 45 minutes.

Roasted Red Pepper Chicken

The roasted peppers in this recipe make the flavor truly worth the effort.

Ingredients:

- 4   skinless boneless chicken breasts
- 1   can roasted red bell peppers (12 oz.)
- 2   c. bread crumbs, dried
- 2   tsp. Italian seasoning
- 3   Tbs. canola oil
- 1   c. sour cream
- ½   c. feta cheese

Directions:

1. With a very sharp knife, cut pockets into the thickest part of the breast of chicken.
2. Stuff as many pieces of roasted red peppers as you can into pockets of chicken, one at a time.
3. In large plastic bag, pour bread crumbs and Italian seasoning.
4. Place chicken breasts in bag; shake until well coated.
5. In large skillet, on medium-high, heat oil and place chicken in the skillet.
6. Cook for 5 minutes on one side, then turn and cook for 10 minutes on the other side.
7. While cooking the chicken, blend sour cream and a few pieces of red peppers in an electric blender.
8. Turn chicken one more time and cook 5 more minutes, or until chicken is done.
9. Cut each piece of chicken in half and arrange the pieces on a plate.
10. Drizzle with sour cream mixture, and sprinkle with feta cheese before serving.

Valentine Delights Cookbook
A Collection of Valentine Recipes
Cookbook Delights Holiday Series - Book 2

Pies

Table of Contents

Page

A Basic Recipe for Pie Crust

This is a very good recipe for a delicious, flaky crust.

Ingredients for single crust:

    1½ c. sifted all-purpose flour
    ½   tsp. salt
    ½   c. shortening
    4-5 Tbs. ice water

Ingredients for double crust:

    2   c. sifted all-purpose flour
    1   tsp. salt
    ⅔   c. shortening
    5-7 Tbs. ice water

Directions for single crust:

1. In large bowl stir together flour and salt.
2. Cut in shortening with pastry blender or mix with fingertips until pieces are size of coarse crumbs.
3. Sprinkle 2 tablespoons ice water over flour mixture, tossing with fork.
4. Add just enough remaining water 1 tablespoon at a time to moisten dough, tossing so dough holds together.
5. Roll pastry into 11-inch circle, and wrap in plastic wrap; refrigerate for 1 hour.
6. Preheat oven to 425 degrees F.
7. Remove plastic wrap from pastry, and fit pastry into a 9-inch pie plate.
8. Fold edge under and then crimp between thumb and forefinger to make fluted crust.
9. For filled pie with an instant or cooked filling (cream-filled, custard-filled, etc.), prick crust all over with fork then bake 15 to 20 minutes until done.
10. If preparing pie with uncooked filling (such as pumpkin), do not prick crust; pour filling into unbaked pastry shell, and then bake as directed.

Directions for double crust:

1. Turn desired filling into pastry-lined pie plate; trim overhanging edge of pastry ½ inch from rim of plate.
2. Cut slits with knife in top crust for steam vents.
3. Place over filling; trim overhanging edge of pastry 1 inch from rim of plate.
4. Fold and roll top edge under lower edge, pressing on rim to seal; flute.
5. Cover fluted edge with 2- to 3-inch-wide strip of aluminum foil to prevent excessive browning.
6. Remove foil during last 15 minutes of baking.

Yields: 1 pie crust (9-inch single or double).

A Basic Cookie or Graham Cracker Crust

This is a great crust for use with cream pies or for an unbaked pie. Use your favorite flavor of cookie to complement your filling, or use graham crackers.

Ingredients:

2 c. cookie or graham cracker crumbs, finely crushed
⅓ c. sugar
½ c. butter, melted

Directions:

1. Combine crumbs, sugar, and butter.
2. Press mixture firmly against bottom and up sides of 9-inch pie plate.
3. Baking is not necessary, but if preferred crust may be baked at 400 degrees F. for 10 minutes.

Yields: 1 pie crust (9-inch).

Cherry Pie Supreme

This is a beautiful presentation of an easy-to-make cherry pie for serving on Valentine's Day.

Ingredients:

- 1   pie shell, unbaked (see recipe on page 202)
- 2   c. prepared cherry pie filling, divided
- ½ c. sugar
- 2   lg. eggs
- 1½ pkg. cream cheese, softened (12 oz.)
- ½ tsp. vanilla extract
- 1   c. sour cream

Directions:

1. Preheat oven to 425 degrees F.
2. Pour half of pie filling into prepared pie crust.
3. Bake 15 minutes.
4. Reduce heat to 350 degrees F.
5. In medium bowl, beat sugar, eggs, cream cheese, and vanilla until smooth.
6. Pour over baked pie filling.
7. Bake 25 minutes, or until done in the middle.
8. Cool completely.
9. Spoon remaining filling into middle of the pie.
10. Spoon sour cream around the edge and serve.

Chocolate Cherry Cheesecake

Chocolate and cherries make a great combination and are absolutely delicious in this decadent pie.

Ingredients for crust:

- 11 graham crackers, finely crushed
- ¼ c. sugar

5 Tbs. butter, unsalted, melted
nonstick cooking spray

Ingredients for filling:

6 oz. bittersweet chocolate, coarsely chopped, divided
3 oz. cream cheese, softened
2 lg. eggs
1 c. sugar
2 tsp. vanilla extract
2 c. canned pie cherries, pitted, drained well

Directions for crust:

1. Preheat oven to 350 degrees F.
2. Lightly spray a 9-inch pie pan with cooking spray.
3. In medium bowl, combine graham crumbs, sugar, and melted butter; mix well.
4. Press the crumb crust into the pan; set aside.
5. Place a baking sheet on the center rack.

Directions for filling:

1. In small saucepan, melt 4 ounces of the chocolate; set aside to cool slightly.
2. With electric mixer, combine cream cheese, eggs, sugar, vanilla, and melted chocolate; mix until very smooth.
3. Fold in cherries.
4. Spoon filling into unbaked crust.
5. Place pie in the oven on the baking sheet.
6. Bake 40 minutes, so that the pie will be firm to touch, but still soft in the center.
7. Cool on a rack.
8. Melt remaining 2 ounces of chocolate and drizzle over the pie.
9. Cover loosely and refrigerate at least 4 hours before serving.

Strawberry Flan

This is a variation on a traditional flan, but one which we are sure you will enjoy.

Ingredients for crust:

½ c. butter, softened
2   Tbs. sugar
1   tsp. lemon zest, grated
1⅓ c. flour

Ingredients for filling:

1   c. mascarpone cheese
3   Tbs. powdered sugar
2   tsp. lemon zest, grated
¼   tsp. vanilla extract
¼   c. whipping cream
2   c. sm. strawberries, rinsed, hulled, halved

Ingredients for glaze:

¼   c. red strawberry jelly
1   tsp. lemon juice

Directions for crust:

1. Preheat oven to 400 degrees F.
2. In large bowl, with a mixer, combine butter, sugar, and lemon zest; mix well.
3. Add flour; mix until mixture just starts to cling together.
4. Turn out onto floured surface.
5. Gently knead until mixture forms a ball.
6. Flour fingertips; press dough into 9-inch flan pan.
7. Place in freezer for 20 minutes.
8. Bake 12 minutes, or until golden.
9. Cool completely on wire rack.
10. Set aside.

Directions for filling:

1. In medium bowl, beat together mascarpone cheese, powdered sugar, lemon zest, and vanilla.
2. Add whipping cream; beat until blended.
3. Spread cheese mixture into cooled crust.
4. Top with strawberries in concentric circles.
5. To make glaze: In small saucepan, heat jelly and lemon juice until jelly melts; brush over strawberries.
6. Refrigerate until ready to serve.

Fresh Cherry Pie

Nothing is better than fresh cherry pie. Serve warm with vanilla ice cream or topped with a dollop of sweetened whipped cream.

Ingredients:

4   Tbs. quick cooking tapioca
⅛   tsp. salt
1   c. white sugar
4   c. pie cherries, pitted
¼   tsp. almond extract
½   tsp. vanilla extract
1½ Tbs. butter
1   9-inch double pie crust (see recipe on page 202)

Directions:

1. Preheat oven to 400 degrees F.
2. Place bottom crust in pie pan.
3. Set top crust aside, covered.
4. In large mixing bowl, combine tapioca, salt, sugar, cherries, and extracts; let stand 15 minutes.
5. Turn out into bottom crust and dot with butter.
6. Cover with top crust; flute edges and cut vents in top. Place pie on a foil-lined baking sheet.
7. Bake 50 minutes, or until golden brown.

Chocolate Pie

My mom always used to make this for my dad, and, of course, we all enjoyed it. This is a great treat for chocolate lovers.

Ingredients:

2 c. sugar
5 Tbs. unsweetened cocoa powder
¼ c. flour
1 can evaporated milk
1 tsp. vanilla extract
4 lg. eggs, separated
¼ c. butter
¼ c. sugar
1 9-inch single crust pie (see recipe on page 202)

Directions:

1. Preheat oven to 350 degrees F.
2. In medium saucepan, whisk together sugar, cocoa, and flour.
3. Blend in milk and vanilla.
4. In small bowl, beat egg yolks.
5. Stir into sugar mixture.
6. Over low heat, stirring constantly, heat just until butter is melted.
7. Pour filling into unbaked pie shell.
8. Bake 35 to 40 minutes, or until pie is not wobbly when shaken.
9. In small bowl, beat egg whites until soft peaks form.
10. Gradually add ¼ cup sugar, beating constantly, until stiff peaks form.
11. Spread meringue on pie.
12. Return pie to oven.
13. Bake until meringue is golden.
14. Cut into wedges.

Fresh Sour Cherry Pie

This is a traditional cherry pie that is delicious served with vanilla ice cream or sweetened whipped cream.

Ingredients:

- 4 c. sour or tart pie cherries
- ¼ c. cornstarch
- 2 Tbs. flour
- 1 c. sugar
- 2 drops almond extract
- 1 Tbs. lemon juice
- 1 Tbs. butter, unsalted
- 1 9-inch double pie crust (see recipe on page 202)
    milk or half and half cream, for glazing

Directions:

1. Preheat oven to 425 degrees F.
2. Line a 9-inch pie pan with pastry.
3. In large bowl, combine cherries, cornstarch, flour, sugar, almond extract, and lemon juice.
4. Spoon or mound mixture into unbaked pie shell.
5. Dot with butter.
6. Place second pastry crust on top of pie.
7. Press securely onto edges to seal; trim edges and crimp.
8. Cut slits for steam to escape, and brush with milk or half and half.
9. Place pie on a doubled up baking sheet and place on the lowest rack in the oven.
10. Bake 20 minutes.
11. Reduce heat to 375 degrees F.
12. Continue baking 35 to 45 minutes, or until juices begin to bubble out through steam slits.
13. Cool; cut into wedges.

Twin Peaks Cherry Pie

This is also a traditional version of a cherry pie, the difference being that this one is made with cinnamon to give it a unique taste.

Ingredients:

- 2 cans of tart cherries, drained, pitted, reserve ½ the liquid (16 oz. each)
- 1 c. sugar
- 3 Tbs. cornstarch
- ⅛ tsp. cinnamon
- 1 pinch salt
- 1 Tbs. lemon juice
- ¼ tsp. vanilla extract
- 1 9-inch double pie crust (see recipe on page 202)

Directions:

1. Preheat oven to 425 degrees F.
2. In medium saucepan, combine sugar, cornstarch, cinnamon, and salt.
3. Stir in reserved cherry liquid and lemon juice.
4. Over medium heat, bring to boil, stirring constantly.
5. Boil 1 minute; remove from heat.
6. Stir in cherries and vanilla.
7. Line 9-inch pie plate with pastry.
8. Pour filling into pastry-lined pie plate.
9. Place second pastry over top of the filling and trim edges, then flute.
10. Bake 15 minutes.
11. Reduce heat to 375 degrees F.
12. Bake 30 minutes more, until crust is golden and filling is bubbly.
13. Serve warm, or at room temperature.
14. Cut in wedges; top with vanilla ice cream or a dollop of whipped cream.

Rhubarb Strawberry Pie

This classic dessert is delicious, especially with a scoop of vanilla ice cream!

Ingredients:

- 4 c. fresh or frozen rhubarb, chopped
- 2 c. fresh strawberries, rinsed, hulled, sliced
- 1⅓ c. sugar
- ¼ c. cornstarch
- 1 Tbs. lemon juice
- ¼ tsp. cinnamon
- 1 egg, beaten
- 1 9-inch double pie crust (see recipe on page 202)

Directions:

1. Preheat oven to 425 degrees F.
2. Line a 9-inch pie plate with a single crust leaving a ½-inch overhang.
3. In large bowl, combine rhubarb, strawberries, sugar, cornstarch, lemon juice, and cinnamon.
4. Place mixture in unbaked pie shell.
5. Cut remaining pastry into 1-inch strips.
6. Make a lattice top crust on the pie by crisscrossing the strips over the filling.
7. Trim the strips even with the pie plate.
8. Fold the ½-inch of the bottom crust over the ends of the strips.
9. Seal and flute edges; brush egg over the top.
10. Place on a baking sheet.
11. Bake for 15 minutes.
12. Reduce heat to 375 degrees F.
13. Continue to bake for 50 to 60 minutes, until crust is golden, rhubarb is tender, and filling is thickened.
14. Cool.
15. Cut into wedges.

Strawberry Cream Pie

This pie tastes like a bite of heaven! Serve it chilled, and make sure there is plenty to go around!

Ingredients:

   3 Tbs. cornstarch
   ½ tsp. salt
   ½ c. sugar
   3 Tbs. flour
   2 c. milk
   1 egg, slightly beaten
   1 c. whipping cream, whipped
   1 tsp. vanilla extract
   2 c. fresh strawberries, rinsed, hulled, halved
   ½ c. strawberry jam or preserves
   ½ c. water
   2 tsp. cornstarch
   ¼ c. sugar
   1 pie crust, baked (see recipe on page 202)
       almonds, slivered, toasted

Directions:

1. To make cream filling: In large bowl, combine first 4 ingredients; gradually stir in milk.
2. Stirring constantly, bring to a boil.
3. Reduce heat; cook and stir until thick.
4. Stir a little of the hot mixture into egg; return egg mixture to remaining hot mixture.
5. Bring just to boiling, stirring constantly.
6. Cool, and then chill filling.
7. In medium bowl, beat chilled filling well.
8. Fold in half of the whipped cream and vanilla.
9. Toast almonds until lightly browned, and sprinkle over the bottom of the cooled pie crust.
10. Pour cream filling into almond covered crust.

11. Pile halved strawberries on top of the filling.
12. To make the glaze: In small bowl, mix sugar and cornstarch.
13. Add water, and stir to dissolve cornstarch.
14. Add ½ cup jam to sugar mixture, cook and stir until thickened
15. Cool slightly; pour over strawberries.
16. Keep refrigerated until serving time.
17. Cut into wedges; serve with whipped cream.

Strawberry Pie

This is an easy-to-make pie, which is traditionally a favorite. Serve with a big dollop of sweetened whipped cream.

Ingredients:

1 pkg. wild strawberry gelatin powder (3 oz.)
2 Tbs. cornstarch
1 c. sugar
4 c. strawberries, washed, cut in half
1 c. water, hot
1 basic pastry crust, baked (see recipe page 196))

Directions:

1. In small saucepan, mix gelatin powder, cornstarch, and sugar together.
2. Stir in hot water.
3. Over low heat, cook, stirring constantly, until mixture comes to a boil and thickens.
4. Place prepared strawberries in pie shell.
5. Pour hot mixture over berries.
6. Chill pie in refrigerator for 3 to 4 hours before serving.

Cherry Almond Pie

Almonds and cherries make a nice flavor combination.

Ingredients for filling:

    1½ c. sugar
    4   Tbs. cornstarch
    6   c. pie cherries, pitted
    3   Tbs. almond flavoring
    1   pie shell, baked (see recipe on page 202)

Ingredients for topping:

    ¼   c. flour
    ½   c. sugar
    ¼   c. butter
    ½   c. coconut, shredded or flaked

Directions:

1. Preheat oven to 375 degrees F.
2. To make topping: In medium bowl, combine flour and sugar, cut in butter with pastry cutter until texture of coarse meal.
3. Cut in coconut until all is blended; set aside.
4. In large saucepan, combine sugar and cornstarch.
5. Add cherries and flavoring.
6. Over low heat, cook and stir until mixture thickens.
7. Spoon hot filling into baked pie shell.
8. Sprinkle topping over top of pie from outside edge to within 2 inches of center.
9. Bake 10 to 12 minutes, or until coconut is toasted.
10. Serve warm or cooled.

Did You Know? . . . .

Did you know that Pope Gelasius declared February 14th to be Saint Valentine's Day in 498 A.D.?

Raspberry Pie

This raspberry pie reminds me of a taste of summer and will be a special treat for Valentine's Day.

Ingredients:

6 c. fresh raspberries
¾ c. sugar
2 Tbs. cornstarch
3 drops almond extract
2 Tbs. lemon juice
1 9-inch double pie crust (see recipe on page 202)

Directions:

1. Preheat oven to 425 degrees F.
2. In large saucepan, combine raspberries, sugar, cornstarch, almond extract, and lemon juice.
3. Heat slowly over low heat.
4. Stir gently until the juice flows and the mixture begins to thicken.
5. Remove from heat and let cool.
6. Place bottom crust into 9-inch pie pan.
7. Pour in the raspberry mixture.
8. Dot with butter.
9. Place top crust over pie.
10. Crimp edges and cut slits for steam to escape.
11. Bake 10 minutes.
12. Reduce heat to 375 degrees F.
13. Continue baking for 30 minutes, covering with tinfoil for the last 10 minutes of baking time.
14. Remove tinfoil.
15. Cool.
16. Cut into wedges.
17. Serve with a dollop of whipped cream, or serve lukewarm with vanilla ice cream.

Rhubarb Custard Pie

This pie is delicious. The sweetness of the custard and the tartness of the rhubarb make a great combination.

Ingredients for pie:

- 4 eggs, slightly beaten
- 6 Tbs. milk
- 2 c. sugar
- ¼ c. flour
- 4 c. fresh rhubarb, cleaned, sliced into 1-inch pieces
- 1 double pie crust (see recipe on page 202)

Directions for filling:

1. Preheat oven to 375 degrees F.
2. Line pie pan with bottom pastry leaving a ½-inch overhang.
3. In large bowl, combine eggs and milk.
4. Stir in sugar and flour.
5. Add rhubarb; mix well.
6. Pour into prepared pan.
7. Cut remaining pastry into 1-inch strips.
8. Make a lattice top crust on the pie by crisscrossing the strips over the filling.
9. Trim the strips even with the pie plate.
10. Fold the ½-inch of the bottom crust over the ends of the strips; seal and flute the edges.
11. Bake 50 to 60 minutes, or until nicely browned.

Did You Know? . . . .

Did you know that some people believed that if a woman saw a robin flying overhead on Valentine's Day, it meant she would marry a sailor? If she saw a sparrow, she would marry a poor man and be very happy. If she saw a goldfinch, she would marry a very rich person.

Valentine Delights Cookbook
A Collection of Valentine Recipes
Cookbook Delights Holiday Series - Book 2

Preserving

Table of Contents

Page

A Basic Guide for Canning, Dehydrating, and Freezing

1. Wash jars in hot, soapy water inside and out with brush or soft cloth.
2. Run your finger around rim of each jar, discarding any with cracks or chips.
3. Rinse well in clean, clear, hot water, using tongs to avoid burns to hands or fingers.
4. Place upside down on clean cloth to drain well.
5. Place lids in boiling water for 2 minutes to sterilize and keep hot until placing on rim of jar.
6. Immediately prior to filling jars with hot food, immerse in hot bath for 1 minute to heat jars. Heating jars avoids breakage.
7. If filling with room-temperature food, you need not immerse immediately prior to filling.
8. Fill jars with food to within ½ inch of neck of jars.
9. When ladling liquid over food, fill jars to 1 inch from rim. This leaves air allowance for sealing purposes.
10. Wipe rims of jars with clean, damp cloth to remove any particles of food, and check again for any chips or cracks.
11. Using tongs, place lids from hot bath directly onto jars.
12. Place rings over the lids, and using a cloth, gloves, or holders, tighten down firmly while hanging onto jars.
13. Do not tighten lids down too hard as air may become trapped in jars and prevent them from sealing.
14. For fruits, tomatoes, and pickled vegetables, place jars into water bath canning kettle so water covers jars by at least 1 inch.
15. For vegetables, process in pressure canner according to manufacturer's directions.
16. Follow time recommended for food being canned.
17. Do not mix jars of food in same canning kettle as times may vary for each kind of food.

18. At end of time recommended for canning, gently lift each jar out of bath with tongs, and place on protected surface.
19. Turn lids gently to be sure they are firmly tight.
20. Place filled, ringed jars on cloth to cool gradually.
21. Do not disturb rings, lids, or jars until sealed. Lids will show slight indentation when sealed.
22. Leave overnight until thoroughly cooled.
23. When cooled, wipe jars with damp cloth, and then label and date each jar.
24. Store upright on shelf in cool, dark place.

Dehydrating

1. Always begin with fresh, good quality food that is clean and inspected for damage.
2. Pretreatment before drying is not necessary, but food that is blanched will keep its color and flavor better. Use same blanching times as you would for freezing. Fruit, especially, responds well to pretreatment.
3. Doing some research on pretreatments may help you decide what procedure you would like to use.
4. You can marinate, salt, sweeten, or spice foods before you dehydrate them.
5. Jerky is meat that has been marinated and/or flavored by rubbing spices into it; avoid oil or grease of any kind as it will turn rancid as the food dries.
6. Vegetables and fruit can be treated the same way.
7. Slice or dice food thin and uniform so that it will dehydrate evenly. Uneven thicknesses may cause food to spoil because thicker parts did not dry as thoroughly as thinner parts.
8. Space food on dehydrator tray so that air can move around each piece.
9. Try not to let any piece touch another.
10. Fill trays with all the same type of food as different foods take different amounts of time to dry.

11. You can, of course, dry different types of food at the same time, but you will have to remember to watch and remove the food that dehydrates more quickly. You can mix different foods in the same dehydrator batch, but do not mix strong vegetables like onions and garlic as other foods will absorb their taste while they are dehydrating.

12. The smaller the pieces, the faster a food will dehydrate. Thin leaves of spinach, celery, etc., will dry fastest. Remove them from the stalks before drying them or they will be overdone, losing flavor and quality. In very warm areas, they might even scorch. If they do, they will taste just like burned food when you rehydrate them.

13. Dense food like carrots will feel very hard when they are ready. Others will be crispy. Usually, a food that is high in fructose (sugar) will be leathery when it is finished dehydrating.

14. Remember that food smells when it is in the process of drying, so outdoors or in the garage is an excellent place to dry a big batch of those onions!

15. Always test each batch to make sure it is "done."

16. Finished food may be pasteurized by putting it in a slow oven (150 degrees F.) for a few minutes.

17. Let food cool before storing.

18. Store in airtight containers to guard against moisture. Jars saved from other food work well as long as they have lids that will keep moisture out.

19. Zip-closure food storage bags work well.

20. Jars of dehydrated carrots, celery, beets, etc., may look cheerful on your countertop, but the color and flavor will fade. Dehydrated food keeps its color and flavor best if stored in a dark, cool place.

21. Dehydrating food takes time, so do not rush it. When you are all done, you will have a dried food stash to be proud of!

Freezing

1. Wash all containers and lids in hot, soapy water using soft cloth.
2. Rinse well in clear, clean, hot water.
3. Cool and drain well.
4. Place food into container to within 1 inch of rim. This allows for expansion of food during freezing.
5. Wipe rim of container with clean, damp cloth, checking for chips or breaks.
6. Be certain cover fits the container snugly to avoid leaks. Burp air from container.
7. If food is hot when placed in container, cool prior to placing in freezer.
8. Label and date each container.
9. Store upright in freezer until frozen solid.

Citrus Strawberry Preserves

These strawberry preserves have just a hint of lemon, lime, and orange flavor added to them with the pieces of the peel added in, and are absolutely delicious.

Ingredients:

> 5 c. strawberries, cut into sm. pieces before measuring
> 1 sm. lemon
> 1 sm. lime
> 1 sm. orange
> 5 c. sugar
> 1 pouch liquid fruit pectin

Directions:

1. Place strawberries into a large saucepan.
2. Remove skins in quarters from lemon, lime, and orange.
3. Lay skins flat.
4. Shave off and discard about half of the white membrane.
5. With a sharp knife or scissors, slice remaining rind very fine.
6. Add to strawberries in saucepan.
7. Add sugar to fruit and mix well.
8. Let stand for 10 minutes.
9. Place saucepan over high heat.
10. Bring to full rolling boil.
11. Boil hard for 5 minutes, stirring constantly.
12. Remove from heat.
13. Immediately stir in liquid fruit pectin.
14. Stir and skim foam for 7 minutes to prevent floating fruit.
15. Process following A Basic Guide for Canning, Dehydrating, and Freezing on page 218.

Watermelon Rind Pickles

My aunt used to make watermelon pickle and they are delicious. They are great to have on hand to add color to a meal for a special occasion, and they also make wonderful gifts.

Ingredients:

1½ qt. watermelon rind, cubed
3   qt. water, divided
3   Tbs. salt
8   c. sugar
1   pt. cider vinegar
2   Tbs. whole cloves
2   Tbs. whole allspice
6   cinnamon sticks (each 3-inch pieces)

Directions:

1. Use rind from a firm, not overripe watermelon.
2. Trim off green skin and pink flesh, leaving only the white rind; cut rind into 1-inch cubes.
3. In large pot, combine 1 quart of water, salt, and rind; let sit overnight.
4. In the morning drain, and cover with fresh water.
5. Boil together remaining water, sugar, and vinegar for 5 minutes.
6. Tie spices in cheesecloth bag.
7. Add rind.
8. Cook, uncovered, until transparent, about 45 minutes.
9. Remove spice bag.
10. Pack in clean, hot, canning jars.
11. Process following A Basic Guide for Canning, Dehydrating, and Freezing on page 218.

Yields: 2 pints.

Five Fruit Cranberry Relish

This makes a wonderful relish that everyone will enjoy.

Ingredients:

- 2 lg. oranges
- 12 oz. fresh cranberries
- 1 can pineapple chunks, drained (20 oz.)
- 1 can pear halves, drained (16 oz.)
- 1 c. seedless raisins
- ½ c. sugar

Directions:

1. About 1½ hours before serving, or a day ahead, cut each unpeeled orange into 3 pieces, discarding any seeds.
2. Cut pineapple chunks and pear halves into ½-inch pieces.
3. In a food processor with knife blade attached, blend oranges and cranberries until coarsely chopped; pour into large bowl.
4. Stir in raisins, sugar, pineapple, and pear pieces.
5. Cover; refrigerate 1 hour, preferably overnight or longer.
6. Spoon into clean, sterilized jars; cover tightly.

Easy Pickled Peppers

This is an easy recipe, and it makes great pickled peppers.

Ingredients:

- 1½ lb. fresh, red or jalapeño peppers (any type)
- 1 handful cayenne peppers
- 1 lb. baby carrots, peeled, sliced
- 1-2 heads garlic, peeled, separated

¼ c. salt
¼ c. black peppercorns
¼ c. whole coriander seeds
　　white vinegar, to cover

Directions:

1. In medium saucepan, add carrots and cover with vinegar; bring to boil and cook for 10 minutes.
2. Stab each pepper with a paring knife.
3. Add remaining ingredients to the carrot mixture.
4. Over low heat, simmer 5 (for crisp) to 15 (for soft) minutes, depending on your taste.
5. Pour mixture into a large glass jar that has a cover, or use several smaller jars with covers.
6. Cool for 1 hour; refrigerate.
7. Note: For larger amounts, process following A Basic Guide for Canning, Dehydrating, and Freezing on page 218.

Canned Tomatoes

Bright red tomatoes are always nice to have on the shelf and can be used in many ways throughout the year.

Ingredients:

1½ tsp. salt
1 qt. tomatoes, rinsed clean
2 qt. water, boiling

Directions:

1. In large pot, drop tomatoes in boiling water for 1 minute; remove and set in colander. Skins should slip off easily at this point.
2. After skins are removed, drop tomatoes in boiling water again. Boil for 3 minutes.
3. Put tomatoes in jars, and process following A Basic Guide for Canning, Dehydrating, and Freezing on page 218.

Strawberry and Banana Fruit Leather

This fruit leather is full of vitamins and has no added chemicals or dyes. It makes a great treat.

Ingredients:

    1 lg. banana, peeled
    2 c. fresh strawberries, rinsed, hulled, patted dry

Directions:

1. In blender, purée banana and strawberries together.
2. Line a 9 x 13-inch tray with plastic.
3. Spread the puréed fruit on the tray making the edges thicker than the middle.
4. Microwave 5 minutes on medium; let sit 2 hours or until dry.
5. Slice into 3-inch wide strips and roll up each strip.
6. Fruit leather rolls may be stored when dry by wrapping in plastic wrap.
7. Store in a cool, dry place.

Dried Cherry Chutney

This is a nice chutney to use when serving poultry or pork dishes, and it also keeps for several weeks in the refrigerator.

Ingredients:

    2   c. cherries, dried, pitted
    1¼ c. sugar
    ¾   c. white vinegar
    ¼   c. celery, finely chopped
    ¼   c. fresh ginger, minced
    6   Tbs. apple juice
    3   Tbs. fresh lemon juice

½ tsp. crushed, dried, red pepper flakes

Directions:

1. In a microwave-safe 2-quart casserole or mixing bowl, combine all ingredients; stir well.
2. Cook, uncovered, on high power for 6 minutes.
3. Stir, until sugar has dissolved; return to microwave.
4. Cook another 8 minutes.
5. Cool to room temperature.
6. Pour into sterilized jars.
7. Cover tightly and refrigerate.

Rhubarb and Fig Preserves

Some of my children love figs, and all of our family loves rhubarb. Together, rhubarb and figs make great preserves.

Ingredients:

3½ qt. rhubarb, cut into sm. pieces
8 c. sugar
1 pt. figs, chopped
1 lemon, juiced, rind cut into pieces

Directions:

1. In large bowl, combine rhubarb and sugar; let stand overnight.
2. In large saucepan, place rhubarb-sugar mixture.
3. Bring to boil; boil until thick,
4. Add figs, lemon juice and rind.
5. Cook rapidly until mixture is thick and clear.
6. Pack while hot into sterilized, hot jars.
7. Process following A Basic Guide for Canning, Dehydrating, and Freezing on page 218.

Spiced Pickled Beets

Try this recipe for pickled beets, it is delicious. You may omit the cinnamon and cloves if you prefer.

Ingredients:

2 c. sugar
2 c. water
2 c. vinegar
1 tsp. ground cloves
1 tsp. allspice
1 Tbs. cinnamon
4 lb. sm. beets

Directions:

1. In large pot, cook beets with roots (about 2 inches of stem) until tender, using enough water to cover. Skins should slip off easily when beets are cooked.
2. After cooking, place in large pan of cool water while slipping skins off.
3. Slice or quarter beets after peeling.
4. In large pot, combine sugar, spices, vinegar, and beets; simmer 15 minutes.
5. Pack beets into hot, sterilized jars and cover with boiling hot syrup to within ½-inch of the rim.
6. Process following A Basic Guide for Canning, Dehydrating, and Freezing on page 218.

Ripe Watermelon Preserves

This is a sweet and delicious preserve.

Ingredients:

4 qt. red watermelon flesh, diced, seeded
5 c. sugar
¼ tsp. salt
½ c. cider vinegar

2 lemon slices
1 tsp. cracked cinnamon
1 tsp. ground cloves

Directions:

1. Place melon in colander; using your hands, squeeze out as much juice as possible. Let drain for 1 hour.
2. In large, heavy kettle, add melon, sugar, salt, vinegar, and lemon.
3. Tie spices up in cheesecloth bag; add to kettle.
4. Over low heat, cook until soft.
5. Pack while hot into sterilized, hot jars.
6. Process following A Basic Guide for Canning, Dehydrating, and Freezing on page 218.

Strawberry Fig Preserves

My daughter Brianne and my son Devontay love figs. This makes a tasty fig preserve that is great on toast or English muffins.

Ingredients:

3 c. figs, mashed
3 c. sugar
1 pkg. strawberry gelatin powder (3 oz.)
¾ c. water

Directions:

1. In Dutch oven, combine figs, sugar, gelatin, and water.
2. Over medium-high heat, bring to slow boil; reduce heat.
3. Simmer 10 minutes; stirring constantly.
4. Place in hot, sterilized jars.
5. Process following A Basic Guide for Canning, Dehydrating, and Freezing on page 218.

Spiced Pickled Pears

For those of you who love pears, do try these. They are tasty and also make a great gift.

Ingredients:

    30 sm. pears
    2   c. vinegar
    3   sticks cinnamon
    1   Tbs. whole allspice
    4½ c. sugar
    1   c. water
    1   tsp. whole cloves

Directions:

1. Wash pears and scrape out blossom end, leave stems intact.
2. Prick skins several times with a fork.
3. Place in large saucepan.
4. Pour in enough boiling water to cover.
5. Cook for 10 minutes; drain.
6. In large saucepan, add sugar, vinegar, water, and spices.
7. Bring to boil.
8. Boil for 5 minutes.
9. Place pears in sugar mixture.
10. Let stand overnight.
11. The next day, drain off the syrup and reserve.
12. Pack pears into 3 or 4 sterilized jars.
13. Place the syrup in a saucepan.
14. Bring to boiling point again.
15. Pour over pears.
16. Process following A Basic Guide for Canning, Dehydrating, and Freezing on page 218.
17. Let stand several weeks before using.

Valentine Delights Cookbook
A Collection of Valentine Recipes
Cookbook Delights Holiday Series - Book 2

Salads

Table of Contents

Page

Salad with Raspberry Vinaigrette

This is a very light salad, perfect for accompanying a heavier meal. Toss just before serving to keep the greens as fresh as possible.

Ingredients:

    4 c. baby lettuce leaves
    4 Tbs. raspberry vinegar
    2 Tbs. olive oil
    2 Tbs. rich vegetable stock
    1 tsp. oregano, chopped
    1 tsp. chives, chopped
        black pepper, to taste

Directions:

1. In small bowl, stir together oil, vinegar, and vegetable stock.
2. Add herbs as close to serving as possible.
3. Toss with baby lettuce and serve.

Confetti Chicken Salad

This colorful and healthy salad is perfect for a light luncheon or as a dinner salad when you are looking for a light meal.

Ingredients:

    1 ripe avocado, cut into ¼-inch cubes
    1 Tbs. fresh lemon juice
    1 c. chicken, cooked, chopped
    1 each, red, yellow, and green bell peppers, seeded, coarsely chopped
    1 ripe tomato, seeded, coarsely chopped
    1 sm. zucchini, unpeeled, coarsely chopped

½ seedless cucumber, unpeeled, coarsely chopped
2 Tbs. fresh parsley, chopped
2 scallions, thinly sliced on diagonal
2 Tbs. olive oil
1 Tbs. red wine vinegar
½ tsp. sugar
   salt and black pepper, to taste

Directions:

1. In small bowl, toss avocado with lemon juice.
2. In large bowl, combine avocado with lemon, chicken, peppers, tomato, zucchini, cucumber, parsley, and scallions.
3. In small bowl, whisk together oil, vinegar, sugar, salt, and pepper.
4. Pour over salad and toss well.
5. Season to taste, and serve immediately.

Double Raspberry Salad

This recipe is easy to make and very tasty. It is a nice beginning to any meal featuring pork or poultry.

Ingredients:

1 pkg. raspberry gelatin powder (3 oz.)
1 c. water, boiling
1 sm. pkg. frozen raspberries
1 can whole cranberries

Directions:

1. In large bowl, dissolve gelatin powder in boiling water.
2. Mix in frozen raspberries and cranberries.
3. Chill until firm.
4. Serve on lettuce-lined salad plates.

Strawberry Salad Platter

This is a nice salad that combines flavors and textures, resulting in a dish that is pleasing to the palate.

Ingredients for salad:

- 3 lg. strawberries, rinsed, hulled, sliced
- 1 sm. sweet red or white onion, thinly sliced
- ¼ sm. jicama, peeled, cut into thin strips 2 inches long
- 1¼ c. fresh basil leaves, lightly packed, snip of stems
- ½ c. pine nuts, toasted

Ingredients for poppy seed dressing:

- 2 Tbs. dry mustard
- 2 Tbs. poppy seeds
- ½ tsp. salt
- ¼ tsp. black pepper, ground
- ¼ tsp. paprika
- 2 Tbs. plus 1 tsp. sugar
- ½ c. organic canola oil
- ⅓ c. apple cider vinegar
- ¼ c. lemon juice
- ¼ c. water

Directions for dressing:

1. Combine all ingredients in a jar and shake well.
2. Refrigerate.
3. Keeps well for 2 weeks.

Directions for salad:

1. In large mixing bowl, combine all salad ingredients.
2. Toss with poppy seed dressing and spoon out onto an attractive serving platter.

Strawberry Salad

Our family loves poppy seeds, and this combination makes a delightful salad.

Ingredients:

1 pt. fresh or frozen strawberries, rinsed, hulled, sliced
1 head romaine, or red tipped lettuce
1 red onion, thinly sliced
½ c. mayonnaise
2 Tbs. strawberry vinegar, or light red wine vinegar
⅓ c. sugar
¼ c. whole milk
4 Tbs. poppy seeds

Directions:

1. If using frozen berries, partially thaw before slicing.
2. Wash lettuce; spin or pat dry.
3. Place in large bowl and cover.
4. Refrigerate until serving time.
5. In shaker jar, place remaining ingredients.
6. Cover and shake until well blended.
7. Chill in refrigerator until just before serving time.
8. When ready to serve, place greens on individual salad plates or in a large salad bowl.
9. Arrange berries and onion slices on top of greens.
10. Drizzle dressing over top of each individual serving, or if using a large salad bowl, pour over salad and toss lightly.
11. Serve this delicious salad as a side dish with your favorite meal, or with fresh bread or rolls.

Yields: 4 to 6 servings.

Cherries Valentine

This is a wonderful fruit salad perfect for a light start to a meal. It also can be used in place of a dessert for those who are calorie conscious.

Ingredients:

　　1½ c. fresh cherries, pitted
　　2　peaches, skinned, halved, pitted
　　2　oranges, juiced or ½ c. orange juice
　　4　orange wedges
　　4　whole cherries with stems

Directions:

　　1. In blender, add cherries, peaches, and orange juice.
　　2. Blend at medium speed until creamy.
　　3. Pour mixture into custard glasses.
　　4. Top each glass with an orange wedge and whole cherry.
　　5. Serve immediately.

Seafood Salad

This salad makes a great main dish for a brunch or light luncheon.

Ingredients:

　　1　lb. fresh crabmeat
　　1　lb. shrimp, boiled, shells removed, deveined
　　1　head curly leaf lettuce, torn into bite-size pieces
　　½　green pepper, thinly sliced
　　2　green onions, finely chopped
　　1　avocado, peeled, sliced
　　½　c. ripe olives
　　12 cherry tomatoes

2   eggs, hard-boiled, sliced into quarters
1   pimento, thinly sliced

Directions:

1. In large serving bowl, place lettuce pieces in it.
2. Scatter shrimp and crabmeat onto the lettuce and garnish with remaining ingredients.
3. Chill thoroughly.
4. Pour a generous amount of your favorite seafood sauce or salad dressing over the salad just prior to serving.

Raspberry Spinach Salad

The fruity flavor of the raspberries makes the strong flavor of the spinach more subtle, and the nuts give this salad the texture it needs.

Ingredients:

2 Tbs. raspberry vinegar
2 Tbs. raspberry jam
⅓ c. olive oil
8 c. fresh spinach, rinsed, stemmed, torn into pieces
¾ c. macadamia nuts, coarsely chopped
1 c. fresh raspberries
3 kiwis, peeled, sliced

Directions for dressing:

1. In blender or small bowl, combine vinegar and jam.
2. Add oil in thin stream, blending well.
3. In large salad bowl, toss spinach with half of the nuts, half of the raspberries, half of the kiwis, and the dressing.
4. Garnish with the remaining nuts, raspberries, and kiwis.

Valentine's Day Salad

The combination of fruits, along with the pink and white colors in this salad makes it a great choice for a Valentine's Day dish.

Ingredients:

> 2 pkg. strawberry flavored gelatin powder (3 oz. ea.)
> 2 c. water, boiling
> 1 pkg. frozen strawberries, partially thawed
> 2 bananas, peeled, sliced
> 1 can pineapple, crushed, well drained (20 oz.)
> 1 c. frozen whipped topping
>   lettuce leaves

Directions:

1. In medium saucepan, over high heat, bring to boil; stir in gelatin.
2. Remove from heat; stir until gelatin is dissolved.
3. Add strawberries, bananas, and pineapple; mix well.
4. Spoon into individual heart molds or 9 x 13-inch baking dish.
5. Chill until firm; unmold.
6. Serve on lettuce-lined plates or serving plate.
7. Top with dollops of whipped topping.

Cranberry Orange Salad

This is a flavorful gelatin salad, and you may omit the walnuts if you prefer. It will still be just as tasty.

Ingredients:

> 3½ c. cranberry juice cocktail
> 1   lg. pkg. orange flavor gelatin (6 oz.)
> 1½ c. frozen or fresh cranberries, chopped
> ½   c. walnuts, chopped
> 11 oz. mandarin orange segments, drained
>   sweetened whipped cream, for garnish

Directions:

1. In small saucepan, bring 1½ cups cocktail to a boil.
2. In large bowl, dissolve gelatin in hot cocktail.
3. Stir in remaining 2 cups of cocktail.
4. Refrigerate until thickened but not set, about 1 hour.
5. Lightly oil a 6-cup ring or other mold.
6. Stir cranberries, walnuts, and orange segments into thickened gelatin.
7. Spoon into oiled mold.
8. Refrigerate until firm, about 4 hours.
9. To serve, line serving plate with lettuce leaves.
10. Unmold gelatin onto serving plate.

Sweetheart Broccoli Salad

The combination of flavors and textures in this salad are delightful, and it will make you want more.

Ingredients for salad:

1   pkg. frozen broccoli florets
2   red bell peppers
¼ c. cranberries, sweetened, dried
¼ c. sunflower seeds, salted, shelled

Ingredients for dressing:

½ c. Italian salad dressing
3   Tbs. orange marmalade
½ tsp. cumin

Directions:

1. Cook broccoli as directed on package.
2. Drain, and rinse with cold water to cool; drain well.
3. In large bowl, combine broccoli and remaining ingredients.
4. In small bowl, combine dressing ingredients, blend well.
5. Pour dressing over salad, toss until well mixed.
6. Refrigerate at least 20 minutes before serving.

Chicken and Strawberry Salad

This is a savory chicken and strawberry salad that will impress your guests.

Ingredients:

- 4 Tbs. orange juice
- 1 Tbs. olive or canola oil
- 1 Tbs. lemon juice
- 2 tsp. sugar
- ¼ c. soy sauce
- ¼ c. green onions, thinly sliced
- 1 garlic clove, minced
- 12 oz. skinless boneless chicken breasts
- 4 c. spinach leaves
- 1 can mandarin oranges, drained (11 oz.)
- 1 c. strawberries, sliced

Directions:

1. In a screw-top jar, combine 2 tablespoons of orange juice, oil, lemon juice, and sugar.
2. Cover and shake well. Chill until serving time.
3. In small bowl, combine soy sauce, green onions, garlic, and remaining orange juice.
4. Place chicken in a plastic bag set into a shallow dish.
5. Add marinade and seal bag. Turn chicken to coat well.
6. Chill 2 hours, or up to 24 hours, turning chicken occasionally.
7. Remove chicken from bag, reserving marinade.
8. Grill chicken on an uncovered grill directly over medium coals for 5 minutes.
9. Brush chicken with marinade; turn chicken and brush with marinade.

10. Grill 7 to 10 minutes more, or until chicken is tender and no longer pink.
11. Cool slightly and slice chicken breasts.
12. Line four individual salad plates with spinach leaves.
13. Arrange oranges, strawberries, and chicken breast slices on spinach-lined plates.
14. Shake dressing and drizzle over salad.

Rhubarb Cream Cheese Salad

Cream cheese adds a nice contrast to this rhubarb gelatin salad.

Ingredients:

2 c. rhubarb, sliced
½ c. sugar
½ c. water
1 pkg. cream cheese (4 oz.)
1 pkg. orange gelatin (3 oz.)
⅔ c. celery, cut thin
⅔ c. nuts, chopped
   mayonnaise or whipped topping

Directions:

1. In medium saucepan, combine rhubarb, sugar, and water; bring to boil.
2. Cool 10 minutes.
3. Dissolve gelatin and cream cheese in hot rhubarb.
4. Chill mixture until thickened.
5. Whip until fluffy.
6. Add celery and nuts.
7. Chill until firm.
8. When ready to serve, top with ½ cup mayonnaise or whipped topping.

Strawberry Fruit Salad

This is an excellent frozen salad that is versatile enough to be served as a salad or dessert.

Ingredients:

1 pkg. cream cheese, at room temperature (8 oz.)
¾ c. sugar
1 can pineapple, crushed (20 oz.)
10 oz. frozen strawberries
3 bananas, sliced
   frozen dessert topping, thawed

Directions:

1. In medium bowl, soften cream cheese with fork; add sugar and blend well.
2. Stir in pineapple, strawberries, and topping; mix well.
3. Fold in bananas last to maintain shape.
4. Spoon into a 9 x 13-inch pan and freeze 6 to 8 hours.
5. Keep frozen until ready to serve then cut into squares.

Strawberry Ambrosia Salad

Many people have tried different versions of ambrosia. Try this version with colorful strawberries.

Ingredients:

1 lg. can pineapple chunks, drained
1 lg. can peaches, sliced, drained
2 sm. cans mandarin oranges, drained
3 c. whipped cream
1 c. coconut, shredded
½ c. walnuts, chopped

2 c. strawberries, rinsed, hulled, sliced
¼ c. sugar

Directions:

1. In large bowl, combine pineapple, peaches, and mandarin oranges with whipped cream.
2. Gently fold in the walnuts and coconut.
3. Toss strawberries with sugar; fold into the salad.
4. Place in refrigerator and chill until ready to serve.

Yields: 8 to 10 portions.

Springtime Rhubarb Salad

Rhubarb gelatin salad makes a pleasant spring salad.

Ingredients:

2½ c. rhubarb, cut into 1-inch pieces
½ c. water
1 c. sugar
1 Tbs. lemon juice
1 pkg. raspberry flavored gelatin (6 oz.)
½ c. water, boiling
2 c. celery, chopped
1 c. walnuts, chopped

Directions:

1. In medium saucepan, boil rhubarb in water until tender.
2. Add sugar to dissolve.
3. Add lemon juice and chill.
4. In large bowl, dissolve gelatin with boiling water.
5. Cool.
6. Blend all ingredients together and chill.

Salad with Strawberry Vinaigrette

This is another light salad that is a perfect accompaniment to a heavier meal. Fresh strawberries bring the taste of summer to the meal.

Ingredients for vinaigrette:

½ c. fresh strawberries, rinsed, hulled
2 tsp. sugar
¼ tsp. salt
1 dash pepper
1 Tbs. olive oil
2 tsp. balsamic vinegar

Ingredients for salad:

10 oz. romaine blend mixed salad greens
1 c. fresh strawberries, rinsed, hulled, sliced
1 can mandarin orange segments, drained (11 oz.)
1 Tbs. green onions, sliced

Directions:

1. In blender, combine vinaigrette ingredients.
2. Cover, blend until smooth.
3. To assemble salads, divide salad greens onto individual plates.
4. Top each with ¼ cup strawberries and ¼ of the orange segments.
5. Drizzle vinaigrette over salads; sprinkle with green onions.

Did You Know? . . . .

Did you know that the first televised tour of the White House aired on February 14th in 1962? First Lady Jackie Kennedy hosted the tour.

Valentine Delights Cookbook
A Collection of Valentine Recipes
Cookbook Delights Holiday Series - Book 2

Side Dishes

Table of Contents

Page

Cajun Salmon Pasta

This is a delightfully spicy salmon dish, which also includes pasta. Serve it with a green salad, and you will have a wonderful meal.

Ingredients:

    2 thin salmon filets, room temperature
    4 tsp. olive oil
    ½ med. onion, or 4 green onions, sliced
    2 garlic cloves, minced
    ½ med. bell pepper, thinly sliced
    ¼ c. milk
       Cajun seasoning
       pasta, enough for two
       cherry tomatoes, sliced in 2 pieces
       Parmesan cheese, grated

Directions:

1. In medium skillet, add 2 teaspoons olive oil; warm over medium heat.
2. Add onions; stir-fry until they are translucent.
3. Add bell pepper and garlic; stir-fry until vegetables are cooked but not limp.
4. Remove vegetables.
5. Cook pasta according to package directions; drain.
6. Immediately add 1 tablespoon olive oil and stir. Do not let pasta cool.
7. Add 1 teaspoon oil to skillet; heat on medium-high.
8. Pour Cajun seasoning over salmon filets, and drop them in hot skillet (they should smoke).
9. Burner temperature may need adjusting depending on how thick the filets are, and how defrosted. If the outside is browning too rapidly, lower heat to medium to give the inside time to cook.

10. When filets are blackened on one side, pour seasoning on the face up side and flip them over.
11. In small cup, in microwave, heat milk to scalding; pour only as much into pasta as can be absorbed.
12. At same time, stir in 1 teaspoon of Cajun seasoning.
13. When salmon filets are blackened on both sides, remove from heat.
14. Quickly spoon pasta onto two serving plates, top with stir-fried vegetables.
15. Using a wooden spatula, break salmon filets into bite-size chunks and spoon over top of the pasta.
16. Sprinkle grated Parmesan over pasta.
17. Garnish with cherry tomatoes and fresh parsley.

Chipotle Mashed Potatoes

The addition of chipotle peppers and cheese gives a twist to the traditional mashed potatoes.

Ingredients:

6   Tbs. butter
6   Tbs. milk
6   Tbs. Monterey jack cheese, shredded
6-8 med. white potatoes, peeled, cut into chunks
1½ tsp. chipotle peppers in adobo sauce, minced
1   tsp. ground cumin
2   Tbs. cilantro, chopped
     salt and pepper, to taste

Directions:

1. In large saucepan, cook potatoes in salted water until tender; drain and mash.
2. In small bowl, combine butter, milk, cheese, peppers, cumin, and cilantro.
3. Pour into potatoes; mix well.
4. Season with salt and pepper.

Crab Stuffed Potatoes

Crab is a great addition to stuffed potatoes, and gives a new twist to the old standard of twice baked potatoes.

Ingredients:

    4 lg. white potatoes, baked
    4 Tbs. butter
    ½ c. sour cream
    4 tsp. onion, finely chopped
    1 tsp. salt
    ½ lb. crabmeat
    ½ tsp. paprika

Directions:

1. Preheat oven to 350 degrees F.
2. Scoop insides out of potatoes; place in large bowl.
3. With mixer on low speed, beat for 2 minutes; add butter, onion, and salt.
4. Fold in crabmeat; gently put mixture back into potatoes.
5. Sprinkle with paprika.
6. Bake 15 minutes.

Yields: 4 to 8 servings.

Cranberry Sweet Potatoes

This dish is lovely to see on the dinner table, and it's even better to eat.

Ingredients:

    4   med. sweet potatoes, peeled, cut into ¾-inch pieces
    ¼ c. orange juice
    ¼ c. butter

1¼ c. fresh cranberries
¼ c. brown sugar, packed
½ c. almonds, slivered, toasted
zest from ½ an orange

Directions:

1. In large, microwave-safe bowl, combine sweet potatoes, orange juice, and butter.
2. Cover with plastic wrap; heat on high, stirring occasionally, 12 minutes.
3. Stir in cranberries and brown sugar; cover.
4. Heat on high until potatoes are tender and cranberries burst, about 5 minutes.
5. Toss mixture with orange zest; stir in almonds.

Fried Cauliflower with Lemon

Our family enjoys fried cauliflower, and you may also substitute the cauliflower for another vegetable of your preference.

Ingredients:

1 head cauliflower, separated into florets
1 lemon, juiced, divided
3 inches of canola oil
1½ c. flour

Directions:

1. In large pot, add enough water to cook cauliflower and lemon juice; bring to boil.
2. Cook just until tender, but not soft; drain thoroughly.
3. Dredge in flour; deep fry until golden brown.
4. Season to taste.
5. Sprinkle with remaining lemon juice; serve hot.

Potatoes with Tofu Stuffing

We have two vegetarians in the family, and tofu adds protein to baked potatoes. Add your favorite seasoning to taste.

Ingredients:

    4   potatoes, baked
    12 oz. tofu, pressed
    8   oz. cheese, grated or diced
    ½   tsp. salt
    1½ Tbs. butter
    1   onion, minced
    1   Tbs. canola oil
        minced chives, to taste
        pepper, to taste

Directions:

1. Preheat oven to 350 degrees F.
2. Lightly spray or coat a baking sheet with canola oil.
3. Cut potatoes lengthwise and scoop out shells.
4. In large bowl, add 1 cup of potatoes; reserve remainder.
5. Add tofu and cheese; mash together.
6. Season with salt and pepper.
7. Melt butter in skillet; sauté onion until nicely browned. Mix into potato-tofu mixture.
8. Divide mixture among potato shells.
9. Bake 30 minutes, or until nicely browned.

Did You Know? . . . .

Did you know that in the Middle Ages, people believed that the first unmarried person of the opposite sex you met on the morning of St. Valentine's Day would become your spouse?

Red Potatoes with Mushrooms

This is a nice change of pace from the traditional boiled red potatoes.

Ingredients:

2 tsp. Asian sesame oil, divided
2 Tbs. canola oil
1 Tbs. rice wine vinegar
1 tsp. soy sauce
½ tsp. ground ginger
½ tsp. green onions, chopped
1 tsp. sesame seeds
24 red potatoes, whole (2 inches in diameter)
6 oz. shiitake mushrooms, stemmed, chopped

Directions:

1. In small skillet, heat 1 teaspoon of sesame oil over low heat.
2. Add mushrooms, cook covered, 5 minutes, or until mushrooms are soft.
3. In bowl, whisk together remaining oil, canola oil, rice vinegar, soy sauce, and ginger.
4. Add mushrooms, onions, and sesame seeds; stir together.
5. In large Dutch oven, in 2 inches of simmering water, cook potatoes, covered, 15 minutes, or until tender. Do not add milk or butter.
6. Cut potatoes in half.
7. With melon baller, scoop out some of the flesh from each half to form a cavity.
8. Fill each cavity with 1 teaspoon of the mushroom mixture.
9. Serve with your favorite meat dish and a salad.
10. Note: Reheat in microwave or oven until hot and serve.

Potato and Cheese Quick Bake

This dish lacks the potato skins but is about the same thing as a stuffed potato, without all the work.

Ingredients:

1 lb. potatoes, peeled, quartered
4 egg yolks
1½ c. milk
1¼ cheese, grated
4 egg whites, beaten until stiff
salt and pepper, to taste

Directions:

1. Preheat oven to 350 degrees F.
2. Lightly butter an ovenproof baking dish.
3. In large saucepan, cook potatoes in salted water until tender; drain and mash. Do not add milk or butter.
4. Stir in egg yolks, milk, cheese, and salt and pepper.
5. Fold in beaten egg whites.
6. Place the potato mixture in prepared baking dish.
7. Bake 60 minutes, or until golden brown.

Creamy Mushroom Potato Bake

This is a nice variation on the traditional dish of scalloped potatoes, and it goes well with steak or any meat that is without its own sauce or gravy.

Ingredients:

3 lb. white potatoes, peeled
1 med. onion, finely chopped
½ lb. fresh mushrooms, chopped
4 Tbs. butter
½ c. sour cream
½ tsp. salt

¼   tsp. pepper
½   c. Parmesan cheese, grated

Directions:

1. In large Dutch oven, cook potatoes in salted water until tender; drain and mash. Do not add milk or butter.
2. Preheat oven to 400 degrees F.
3. Lightly grease a 2-quart baking dish.
4. In a skillet, sauté onion and mushrooms in 2 tablespoons butter, 3 to 4 minutes, or just until tender.
5. Stir onion and mushroom mixture into potatoes along with sour cream, salt, and pepper.
6. Spoon into prepared baking dish.
7. Sprinkle with cheese and remaining butter.
8. Bake, uncovered, 20 to 25 minutes, or until heated through and golden brown.

Wasabi Mashed Potatoes

Wasabi adds just a hint of spicy flavor to plain potatoes. Be sure to use just the amount of Wasabi indicated, as any more will overpower the potato.

Ingredients:

3 lg. white or red potatoes, unpeeled
6 Tbs. nonfat milk
2 Tbs. prepared wasabi paste
2 Tbs. fresh chives, minced
   salt and pepper, to taste

Directions:

1. In medium saucepan, boil potatoes until tender.
2. Mix in milk, wasabi, and chives.
3. Season with salt and pepper.
4. Serve.

Valentine's Rice

This is a slightly sweet dish that makes the taste buds sing. Served alongside baked chicken or pork chops, it makes a wonderful addition to a meal.

Ingredients:

    2 c. rice, cooked, hot
    1 can mandarin oranges, drained, chopped (11 oz.)
    1 c. pineapple, crushed, drained
    ½ c. red pepper, chopped
    ½ c. almonds, slivered, toasted
    ½ c. coconut, unsweetened, grated, toasted
    ⅓ c. green onions, sliced
    2 Tbs. mango chutney
    ¼ tsp. ground ginger

Directions:

1. In large skillet, over medium heat, combine rice, oranges, pineapple, red pepper, almonds, coconut, green onions, chutney, and ginger.
2. Stir and cook until ingredients are blended and thoroughly heated.
3. Serve.

Potato and Tomato Bake

Potatoes and tomatoes make a great combination and taste delightful as the potatoes soak up the juices and spices in this dish and will need no other topping.

Ingredients:

    4 med. potatoes, peeled, sliced in chunks or thick slices
    2 tomatoes, sliced in chunks or thick slices
    1 onion, sliced in chunks or thick slices
    1 tsp. garlic, crushed
    ¼ tsp. oregano

¼ tsp. rosemary
¼ tsp. thyme
  olive oil
  salt and pepper, to taste

Directions:

1. Preheat oven to 300 degrees F.
2. In large bowl, add potatoes and tomatoes.
3. Add garlic; toss with a good coating of olive oil.
4. Add seasonings and herbs; mix thoroughly.
5. Bake 20 minutes, or until vegetables are cooked through and golden on top, stirring occasionally.

Potato Apple Hash

Potatoes and apples together make an interesting combination. Serve this dish with any poultry or pork dish or as a side dish with a slice of fried ham for breakfast.

Ingredients:

2 Tbs. olive oil
1 sm. onion, diced
2 lg. potatoes, peeled, cored, cut into sm. pieces
2 tart eating apples, peeled, cored, cut into sm. pieces
1 Tbs. fresh thyme leaves
1 Tbs. butter
  salt and pepper, to taste

Directions:

1. In nonstick 12-inch skillet, over medium heat, heat oil.
2. Sauté onions, 5 minutes, or until translucent.
3. Add potatoes, sauté for 10 minutes, or until half cooked.
4. Add apples, thyme, and butter; season with salt and pepper.
5. Cook 10 minutes, or until potatoes are lightly browned and cooked through.

Potatoes Dauphinouise

This fine dish is reminiscent of the classic au gratin potatoes, and very delicious.

Ingredients:

> 4 med. potatoes, peeled, thinly sliced into rounds
> 1 Tbs. butter
> 3 garlic cloves, crushed, finely chopped
> ¼ tsp. nutmeg
> 1 c. cream
> 1 c. milk
> 1 c. Colby, grated, or your favorite cheese
>   salt and fresh ground pepper, to taste

Directions:

1. Lightly butter a baking dish.
2. Line bottom with a single layer of overlapping potato slices.
3. Sprinkle generously with salt, pepper, and nutmeg.
4. Repeat this layering and sprinkling process until you have used all of the potato slices.
5. In large bowl, combine cream and milk; stir well.
6. Pour this mixture over potato slices, gently easing the potato away from the sides of the dish to allow the liquid to penetrate evenly.
7. Place dish onto a microwave-safe plate.
8. Cook, uncovered, in microwave on medium heat for 15 to 20 minutes. Check occasionally.
9. If liquid in potatoes boils over, simply pour it from the plate back into the dish and continue cooking.
10. Microwave just until you can push the blade of a sharp knife through the potato layers without feeling any crunchy resistance.
11. Having reached this stage you can go on to cook the dish in the oven or cover with plastic wrap and keep

in the refrigerator for several hours or even overnight, before cooking.

12. When ready to bake in the oven, preheat your oven to 350 degrees F., and top the potatoes with the grated cheese, then place the dish on an upper shelf in the oven for 20 minutes, or until the top turns golden brown.

13. If you take it from the refrigerator it is going to take longer to cook, so either bring the dish back to room temperature, or add additional time to reheat before topping the potatoes with cheese.

Soft Roasted Vegetables

This is a side dish that will liven up your meal, not only with its color, but also with its savory aroma and flavors.

Ingredients:

4   c. broccoli florets
2   c. yams, trimmed, cut into bite-size pieces
1   c. red onions, peeled, cut into bite-size pieces
1½ Tbs. olive oil
1   tsp. dried Italian herb seasoning
½   tsp. salt
½   tsp. pepper

Directions:

1. Preheat oven to 375 degrees F.
2. Place vegetables in a roasting pan.
3. Add oil, herbs, salt, and pepper.
4. Toss well to mix.
5. Shake roasting pan to scatter vegetables evenly.
6. Roast, turning vegetables with spatula occasionally, for 45 minutes, or until soft and golden brown.

Hot Spiced Strawberries

This is a great side dish when serving pork roast, chicken, or ham.

Ingredients:

1¼ c. apple juice
1   Tbs. cornstarch
½   c. sugar
¼   tsp. ground cloves
¼   tsp. ground nutmeg
¼   tsp. ground cinnamon
1   Tbs. butter
4   c. strawberries, hulled

Directions:

1. Preheat oven to 350 degrees F.
2. In medium saucepan, heat apple juice, cornstarch, and sugar until thickened.
3. Add cloves, nutmeg, cinnamon, and butter, mixing well.
4. Place strawberries in buttered casserole dish.
5. Pour apple juice mixture over strawberries.
6. Bake for 30 minutes, or until bubbling hot.
7. Remove from oven.
8. Place on wire rack for 20 minutes to cool.

Strawberry Fruit Stuffing

This is a delicious side dish and an alternative to classic stuffing.

Ingredients:

3   Tbs. canola oil
1   med. onion, chopped
1   stalk celery, chopped
1   garlic clove, minced
2   Tbs. water

¼ c. strawberry preserves
2½ c. bread crumbs or croutons
¾ c. mixed dried fruit, chopped
2   Tbs. fresh parsley, chopped

Directions:

1. Preheat oven to 350 degrees F.
2. Lightly butter a casserole dish.
3. Heat oil in a large skillet over medium heat.
4. Add onion, celery, and garlic; sauté until soft.
5. Add water and preserves.
6. Remove from heat; stir in bread crumbs, fruit, and parsley.
7. Bake 30 to 45 minutes.
8. Cool 10 minutes on wire rack before serving.

Strawberry Ginger Carrots

This is a new twist on an old favorite vegetable, and it is a delightful one at that!

Ingredients:

1   lb. fresh carrot slices
2   Tbs. strawberry jelly
1½ tsp. butter
¼ tsp. ground ginger
¼ tsp. white pepper
    salt, to taste

Directions:

1. In small saucepan, cook carrot slices until tender but still crisp; drain.
2. In large skillet, heat strawberry jelly, until bubbling and foaming, stirring well.
3. Add butter and ginger, stirring until butter is melted and ginger is well blended.
4. Lightly toss the carrots in the glaze.
5. Season with pepper and salt before serving.

Strawberry Nut Rice

This is an old-fashioned recipe that has been around for ages, and for a good reason – it tastes great!

Ingredients:

2 Tbs. butter
1½ c. celery, chopped
1½ c. onions, chopped
6 c. long-grain white rice, cooked
½ c. raisins
¼ c. honey
2 Tbs. fresh lemon juice
1½ tsp. salt
½ tsp. ground cinnamon
½ tsp. black pepper
⅛ tsp. cayenne pepper
½ c. fresh strawberries, chopped
⅔ c. walnuts or pecans, chopped
¼ c. parsley, chopped

Directions:

1. Preheat oven to 325 degrees F.
2. Lightly butter a baking dish with a cover.
3. In large heavy pot, add butter; cook celery and onions for 5 minutes, or until soft.
4. Add rice and raisins, blending well; let set 15 minutes.
5. Add honey, lemon juice, salt, cinnamon, pepper, and cayenne, blending completely.
6. Lightly fold in strawberries and pecans together.
7. Spoon into prepared dish; cover.
8. Bake 30 minutes.
9. Sprinkle the top with parsley.
10. Serve immediately with your favorite pork, beef, or chicken.

Hot Fruit Casserole

This dish is wonderful as a side dish to serve with roasted meats.

Ingredients:

- 1 can pineapple, sliced, drained
- 1 can apricot halves, drained
- 1 lb. frozen whole strawberries, thawed, drained
- 1 can peach halves in syrup, drained
- ⅓ c. butter
- 2 tsp. curry powder
- 1 c. brown sugar
- 2 Tbs. cornstarch

Directions:

1. Preheat oven to 350 degrees F.
2. Lightly butter a casserole dish.
3. Drain all fruits well, reserving 2 tablespoons pineapple juice.
4. Combine all fruits in prepared dish.
5. In small bowl, mix cornstarch with pineapple juice until cornstarch is dissolved.
6. In small saucepan, melt butter and curry powder together until bubbly.
7. Stir in brown sugar.
8. While stirring continuously, add cornstarch mixture.
9. Cook until thick and bubbly.
10. Drizzle evenly over the drained fruit.
11. Cover.
12. Bake for 45 minutes.
13. Remove from oven place on wire rack.
14. Let stand for 20 minutes.
15. Serve warm or hot with your meal.

Asparagus with Strawberry Vinaigrette

Here is another flavor combination that will make a nice side dish.

Ingredients:

> 2½ lb. asparagus, trimmed, cut stalks into thirds
> 2　c. strawberries, washed, hulled, cut in half
> ¼　c. strawberry vinegar

Ingredients for dressing:

> 1　Tbs. walnut oil
> ½　c. peanut oil
> 1½ tsp. honey

Directions:

> 1.　Steam asparagus until tender, but still crisp.
> 2.　Plunge in ice water; drain.
> 3.　In large bowl, combine strawberries and asparagus.
> 4.　In small bowl, combine dressing ingredients.
> 5.　Toss asparagus and strawberries gently with dressing; chill well before serving.

Strawberry Pecan Stuffing

Try this unique stuffing with its sweet strawberry flavor and pecan-packed crunch.

Ingredients:

> 4　slices day-old bread, cubed
> ½ c. pecans, chopped, toasted
> ½ c. green onions, chopped
> 1　egg, beaten
> 2　Tbs. butter, melted
> 1　tsp. cider vinegar
> 　 salt and pepper, to taste

1 c. fresh strawberries

Directions:

1. Preheat oven to 350 degrees F.
2. Lightly grease a 1-quart baking dish.
3. In large bowl, add bread cubes, pecans, and onions.
4. In small bowl, combine egg, butter, vinegar, salt, and pepper.
5. Pour over bread mixture; toss to combine.
6. Gently fold in strawberries; transfer to prepared dish.
7. Cover; bake 20 to 25 minutes, or until inserted toothpick comes out clean.

Creamed Strawberry Rice

Try this different flavor combination of rice with your favorite meal.

Ingredients:

1 c. strawberries
2 c. white rice
2 c. water, hot
2 c. milk
⅓ c. sugar

Directions:

1. Mash half the strawberries with a fork, reserve remaining strawberries for decorating.
2. Wash rice, drain well.
3. Place rice in shallow dish with water and milk.
4. In microwave, on high heat, cook 20 minutes, or until all liquid is absorbed, stirring occasionally during cooking.
5. Add sugar and strawberries; reheat on high for 2 minutes.
6. Serve hot or cold with cream and strawberries.

Rhubarb Potato Delight

Rhubarb is actually a vegetable and is topped with these potato dumplings in this baked sweet side dish or dessert.

Ingredients:

> 3 c. rhubarb, washed, cut into ½-inch pieces
> ½ c. sugar
> 1 c. flour
> 2 tsp. baking powder
> ¼ tsp. salt
> ¼ c. sugar
> ⅜ c. butter
> 1 c. potatoes, cooked, mashed

Directions:

1. Preheat oven to 400 degrees F.
2. Place rhubarb in a lightly greased 9-inch pie plate.
3. Add sugar; a pinch of salt and dots of butter may be added if desired.
4. Bake for 15 minutes.
5. In medium bowl, combine flour, baking powder, salt, and sugar.
6. Cut in butter.
7. Stir in potatoes.
8. Knead mixture; form into a ball.
9. Place on a lightly floured surface, flatten slightly.
10. Roll out to 1-inch thickness.
11. Cut into rounds with a biscuit cutter.
12. Remove rhubarb from oven; drain off juice and save.
13. Measure ⅓ cup of juice; add to rhubarb.
14. Cover rhubarb with rounds of topping.
15. Bake 15 minutes; until golden brown.
16. Serve hot.

Valentine Delights Cookbook
A Collection of Valentine Recipes
Cookbook Delights Holiday Series - Book 2

Soups

Table of Contents

Page

Black Bean Tomato Soup

This is a hearty soup that is also vegetarian and wonderful as a main dish. Serve it with thick crusty bread and your meal is complete.

Ingredients:

  1   lb. plum tomatoes, halved lengthwise
  1   lg. onion, halved lengthwise, cut into thin wedges
  1   med. carrot, peeled, quartered
  3   lg. garlic cloves, chopped
  1   Tbs. olive oil
  ½   tsp. dried oregano
  2   c. canned vegetable broth, or more if desired
  3¼ c. black beans, cooked
  ½   c. plain yogurt, for garnish

Directions:

  1. Preheat oven to 350 degrees F.
  2. In large roasting pan, combine tomatoes, onion, and carrot.
  3. Add garlic, oil, and oregano; stir to coat vegetables.
  4. Roast until vegetables are brown and tender, stirring occasionally, about 55 minutes.
  5. Transfer vegetables to blender or food processor.
  6. Add 2 cups broth to roasting pan and scrape up any browned bits.
  7. Add broth and 2¼ cups beans to processor.
  8. Purée vegetable mixture until almost smooth.
  9. Transfer soup to heavy large saucepan.
  10. Add remaining 1 cup beans.
  11. Bring to boil.
  12. Reduce heat; simmer 10 minutes, until flavors blend, adding more broth if soup is too thick.
  13. Season with salt and pepper.
  14. Ladle soup into bowls; top with a dollop of yogurt.

Sassy Sweet Strawberry Soup

Enjoy this uniquely flavored strawberry soup. It is the perfect beginning or end to any meal.

Ingredients:

  1½ c. strawberries, diced
  1   Tbs. lemon juice
  2   Tbs. lemon peel, grated
  2   eggs, beaten
  ½   c. sugar
  1   Tbs. vanilla extract
  1   qt. buttermilk
  1   c. strawberry ice cream

Directions:

1. In large bowl, sprinkle strawberries with sugar, lemon juice, and lemon peel.
2. Add eggs, vanilla, and buttermilk.
3. Pour mixture into the bowl of a 9-cup food processor.
4. Add ½ cup of ice cream; blend mixture 1 to 2 minutes until ice cream is blended into the soup and liquid has become frothy. If you do not have a 9-cup processor, blend the soup in equal batches.
5. Transfer soup into a large crystal pitcher.
6. Cover and chill for a minimum of 4 hours.
7. Serve soup in champagne glasses.
8. Garnish with remaining ice cream, mint, and additional zest if desired.

Did You Know? . . . .

Did you know that Alexander Graham Bell applied for his patent on the telephone, an "Improvement in Telegraphy", on Valentine's Day, 1876?

Cheesy White Bean Soup

This is a very flavorful soup. Your family and guests will definitely ask for more, so be sure to make plenty.

Ingredients:

- 2 c. dried cannellini beans, soaked 8 to 12 hours, drained, washed, pick clean for stones
- 1 garlic bulb
- 2 Tbs. plus ½ tsp. olive oil, divided
- 1 lg. onion, chopped
- 60 oz. chicken or vegetable broth
- 1 c. each Cheddar and Monterey jack cheese, shredded

Directions:

1. In large saucepan, place washed beans; add enough water to cover beans by a few inches.
2. Bring to a boil on medium-high heat.
3. Reduce heat to medium low; simmer 30 minutes, or until beans until tender.
4. Let beans cool in their cooking liquid; drain and set aside.
5. Preheat oven to 400 degrees F.
6. Cut off and discard top third of garlic bulb; drizzle with ½ teaspoon of the oil.
7. Wrap loosely in foil; place on baking sheet.
8. Bake 40 minutes or until tender.
9. Cool completely.
10. Squeeze garlic pulp from bulb; set aside.
11. Heat remaining 2 tablespoons oil in large stockpot on medium-high heat.
12. Add onions; cook and stir 8 to 10 minutes, or until tender.
13. Add beans, garlic pulp, and broth; stir until well blended. Bring to a boil.
14. Reduce heat to medium-low; simmer 15 minutes.

15. Add soup, in batches, to blender container; cover.
16. Process until smooth; return to pot.
17. Add cheese; cook on medium heat until cheese is melted and soup is heated through, stirring constantly.

Chocolate Soup

Children especially like this soup, and it is great on a lazy day as a breakfast or brunch dish. Serve it on a weekend, when you have time to enjoy it and feel like a child again.

Ingredients:

½ c. sugar
5 Tbs. flour
2 Tbs. cocoa
4 c. whole milk
3 slices of bread, cubed
¼ c. butter
½ tsp. vanilla extract
dash salt

Directions:

1. In medium saucepan, combine sugar, flour, and cocoa.
2. On medium-high heat, cook and brown, stirring frequently. When browned, reduce heat a little.
3. Add a little milk, stirring until creamy.
4. In another saucepan or in microwave, heat remainder of milk just to boiling point.
5. Slowly add a little at a time to chocolate mixture, until all milk is used up. Stir in vanilla and salt.
6. In small skillet, melt butter.
7. Fry bread cubes until golden brown.
8. Add the toasted bread cubes at serving time.

Sun-Dried Tomato Soup

The sun-dried tomatoes add an extraordinary taste to this classic version of tomato soup.

Ingredients for soup:

   1 qt. whole milk
   1 sm. onion, peeled, stuck with 2 cloves
   6 whole peppercorns
   1 pinch salt
   4 Tbs. rice flour
   4 Tbs. milk, cold
   3 oz. sun-dried tomatoes
   2 c. water

Ingredients for bouquet garni:

   6 fresh parsley stems
   ½ tsp. dried leaf thyme
   ½ bay leaf
     (all herbs tied in a cheesecloth)

Ingredients which are optional:

   6 Tbs. heavy cream
     herbs for garnish (basil, chervil, or parsley), chopped

Directions:

1. In medium saucepan, place milk, onion, pepper-corns, salt, and bouquet garni.
2. Bring slowly to a boil.
3. In small bowl, form smooth paste of rice flour and milk.
4. Put into the just boiling milk mixture; stir briskly until there are no lumps.
5. Simmer over very low heat for 20 minutes.

6. Meanwhile, boil sun-dried tomatoes in 2 cups of water; do not drain.
7. Strain milk mixture; add tomatoes and their liquid, and simmer another 5 minutes.
8. In a blender, in batches, liquefy the soup.
9. Return to the stove and bring just to a boil.
10. Add cream, if desired.
11. Serve hot in bowls.
12. Garnish with minced green herbs.

Strawberry Soup

This makes an attractive colored cold soup that is a nice beginning to a meal.

Ingredients:

3 c. strawberries, sliced
1 c. sugar
½ c. water
1 Tbs. corn starch mixed with 1 Tbs. water
1 c. fresh orange juice
1¼ c. sour cream
    sliced strawberries, for garnish
    mint leaves, for garnish

Directions:

1. In large saucepan, combine strawberries, sugar, and water.
2. Bring to boil and simmer 5 minutes.
3. Stir in corn starch and water mixture, and juice.
4. Bring mixture to boil; cook, stirring constantly, until slightly thickened.
5. Cool 15 minutes.
6. Pour into a blender or food processor and purée.
7. Stir in sour cream, and chill.
8. Serve with sliced strawberries and mint leaves.

Cream of Tomato Soup

This is a homemade version of soup that is much more satisfying than any you can get from a can. My family loves this soup and I serve it with grilled bacon and Cheddar sandwiches to make a meal.

Ingredients:

- 1½ c. carrots, diced
- 1 c. celery, diced
- 1 c. onions, diced
- 1½ tsp. garlic in oil
- 1 gal. water
- 10 oz. tomatoes, diced, in juice
- 2 c. tomato paste
- 3 oz. chicken base
- 2 bay leaves
- 2 tsp. salt
- 2 tsp. seasoned pepper
- 1 tsp. basil leaf
- 1 tsp. dill
- 1 tsp. white pepper
- ⅓ c. sugar
- 2 tsp. lemon pepper seasoning
- 1 c. chicken broth
- ¼ lb. Cheddar cheese
- ½ c. butter
- ½ c. flour
- 1 qt. half and half cream

Directions:

1. In a large stockpot, add carrots, celery, onions, and garlic in oil.
2. Sauté until onions are limp.
3. Add remaining ingredients to water and bring to boil.
4. Reduce heat and simmer for 1 hour.
5. Discard bay leaves.

6. In blender, purée vegetables until smooth; pour back into stockpot.
7. In separate saucepan, melt butter and add flour to make a roux.
8. Blend with wire whisk for 5 minutes.
9. Add roux and cheese to soup.
10. Reduce heat; stir constantly until mixture thickens.
11. Add half and half; whisk until blended.
12. Serve.

Strawberry Cherry Soup

This is a traditional Dutch soup. It is perfect for breakfast on the go, soup alone, or with your favorite main dish.

Ingredients:

½ c. barley
6 c. water
½ c. sugar
1 pkg. frozen strawberries (10 oz.)
½ c. raisins
1 c. pitted cherries

Directions:

1. In large bowl, soak the barley in the water overnight; do not drain.
2. In large saucepan, over low heat, simmer barley for 1 hour.
3. Add sugar, strawberries, and raisins.
4. Simmer for another 30 minutes.
5. Add the cherries.
6. Simmer for another 15 minutes, or until the soup becomes relatively thick.
7. Allow to chill in the refrigerator and serve cold.
8. Note: This soup can be stored for at least one week in the refrigerator.
9. Amounts and types of fruits can be varied.

Pink Fish Soup

This is actually a shrimp and fish soup that gets its pink color from the tomatoes.

Ingredients for stock:

        5 c. water
        2 onions
        1 carrot
        1 Tbs. parsley, chopped
        1 bay leaf
        ¼ tsp. thyme
        6 peppercorns
        ½ tsp. salt
           skin, bones, and head of cod or haddock fish

Ingredients for soup:

        3 Tbs. butter
        1 onion, finely chopped
        2 sm. carrots, finely sliced
        2 leeks, sliced
        1 celery stalk, sliced
        1 garlic clove, crushed
        2 Tbs. flour
        2 Tbs. tomato paste
        1 c. canned tomatoes, pushed through sieve
        1 Tbs. parsley, chopped
        ½ lb. shrimp, cooked, deveined
        1 lb. haddock or cod filets, skin, cut into bite-size
           pieces
           paprika, to taste

Directions for stock:

    1. Refrigerate fish filets while making stock.
    2. Combine all stock ingredients; bring to a boil.
    3. Reduce heat; simmer 30 minutes; strain and reserve.

Directions for soup:

1. In large Dutch oven, add butter, onion, carrot, leek, celery, and garlic.
2. Over low heat, cover, cook 5 minutes.
3. Stir flour into vegetables; blend well.
4. Add tomato paste and tomatoes, stirring until well mixed.
5. Add parsley; cover and cook 10 to 15 minutes.
6. Add strained stock and fish pieces to vegetables.
7. Bring to boil; simmer for 10 minutes.
8. Add shrimp; simmer until heated through.
9. Serve sprinkled with paprika.

Strawberry Wine Soup

This soup has a bit of spunk to it. Try this recipe and enjoy!

Ingredients:

1   qt. strawberries
1   c. sour cream
1   c. sugar
2½ c. water
½   c. red wine
6   strawberries, for garnish

Directions:

1. In blender container, add strawberries and blend until uniform; pour into medium bowl.
2. Add sour cream, sugar, water, and wine; blend well.

Did You Know? . . . .

Did you know England's King Henry VIII was the first to declare February 14th a holiday in 1537?

White Sonoran Menudo

This is a traditional soup that comes from Sonora, Mexico. It is eaten for lunch quite frequently among the country folk, and it is delicious.

Ingredients:

> 1 sm. beef calf's foot, split horizontally, cut into 6 pieces
> 1 sm. head of garlic, unpeeled, cut in half horizontally
> 1 med. white onion, roughly sliced
> 1 Tbs. sea salt
> 2 lb. tripe
> ¾ lb. dried hominy, cooked, flowered
>   water for cooking

Ingredients for topping:

> chile piquin, crumbled
> white onion, finely chopped
> cilantro, roughly chopped
> lime quarters

Directions:

1. In Dutch oven, place calf's foot pieces, garlic, onion, and half the salt.
2. Put the tripe on top with the remaining salt.
3. Cover the pan; over very low heat, simmer 3 hours.
4. Strain the meat, reserving the broth, and cut the tripe into 1½-inch squares.
5. Remove bones from calf's foot; chop flesh roughly.
6. Return the meats to the pan with the broth, flowered hominy, and the hominy cooking water.
7. Taste for salt; continue to cook for 1 hour.
8. Serve in deep bowls with flour tortillas.
9. Pass around the toppings.

Strawberry Coconut Milk Soup

The combination of strawberry and coconut make this a great soup for everyone to enjoy.

Ingredients:

    3 c. white grape juice
    ½ c. sugar
    1 lb. fresh strawberries, hulled, sliced in half
    1 pc. fresh ginger, (1 x 1-inch), peeled, sliced
    ¾ c. coconut milk
    2 c. whipping cream plus extra, for garnish
    1 Tbs. coconut, shredded, toasted
      juice of 1 lemon

Directions:

1. In large saucepan, over medium-high heat, combine grape juice with sugar.
2. Heat until sugar is dissolved.
3. Bring mixture to boil.
4. Add strawberries and ginger.
5. Simmer 1 to 2 minutes.
6. Remove pan from heat.
7. Allow mixture to infuse for 30 minutes.
8. After infusing, remove ginger slices and discard.
9. In blender or food processor, purée mixture until smooth.
10. Pass mixture through a sieve.
11. Add lemon juice.
12. Cool mixture to room temperature.
13. Stir whipping cream and coconut milk into the cooled strawberry mixture.
14. Cover and chill thoroughly.
15. To serve, spoon strawberry soup into bowls.
16. Swirl a little extra cream into each portion.
17. Sprinkle with toasted coconut.

Strawberry Bonbon Soup

Try this unique strawberry bonbon soup. This soup is a favorite of our family. For a festive presentation, serve in a clear glass dessert bowl or a martini glass with a strawberry over the rim.

Ingredients for soup:

> 2 c. strawberries, sliced
> 1 c. plain yogurt
> ¼ c. red grape juice or sweet and fragrant red wine (Muscat)
> 1 Tbs. sugar, or to taste
> sprigs of fresh mint, for garnish
> whole strawberries, for garnish

Ingredients for chocolate sauce:

> 1 oz. unsweetened baking chocolate
> 1 tsp. butter
> 3 Tbs. pure maple syrup
> 1 Tbs. cream or half and half cream

Directions for soup:

1. In blender, add all soup ingredients; purée.
2. Adjust sweetening to taste.
3. Cover; refrigerate 3 hours before serving.

Direction for chocolate sauce:

1. In top pan of double boiler, add chocolate and butter.
2. Stir over simmering water until melted.
3. Remove top pan from double boiler.
4. Whisk in maple syrup and cream until smooth.

5. Serve immediately, or set aside and bring to room temperature.
6. To serve, drizzle a swirl of chocolate sauce over bowls of chilled soup.
7. Garnish with fresh mint and strawberries.
8. Note: This soup and the chocolate sauce will keep in separate, covered containers in the refrigerator for up to 2 days.
9. When chilled, the sauce becomes firm; reheat in the microwave on high for about 30 seconds, or until softened; stir before using.

Yields: 2½ cups or 4 servings.

Strawberry Lime Soup

This is a unique combination of flavors. It is great on a hot summer day.

Ingredients:

2 c. unsweetened strawberries
½ c. water
⅓ c. lime juice from concentrate
⅓ c. sugar
1 container sour cream or yogurt (8 oz.)
strawberries, for garnish

Directions:

1. In blender container, combine strawberries, water, lime juice, and sugar; blend until smooth.
2. Pour into medium bowl.
3. Stir in sour cream; mix well.
4. Chill thoroughly.
5. Garnish with strawberries if desired.

Strawberry Champagne Soup

This soup is unique with its blend of strawberries and champagne. Enjoy!

Ingredients:

   2 pt. fresh ripe strawberries
   2 bottles champagne
     sour cream
     lemon peel, finely grated

Directions:

1. Purée strawberries by pushing them through a sieve. This removes the seeds and skin, so do not use the blender; chill in the refrigerator.
2. In shallow crystal bowls, put an equal amount of cold purée. The bowls should rest on a bed of chopped ice, preferably inside a slightly larger crystal bowl.
3. To serve, pass iced champagne, stirring it into the bowl with the strawberry purée.
4. Note: The champagne must be opened at the table when you are ready for it, so that it is not flat.
5. Add sour cream and lemon peel if desired.

Cream of Carrot Soup

Try this delicious soup to serve with your special dinner on Valentine's Day.

Ingredients:

   3   lb. carrots, peeled, sliced
   ½   c. butter
   4   tsp. sugar
   ½   c. rice, jasmine or basmati preferred
   2½   qt. chicken or vegetable stock
   2   tsp. fresh ginger
   1   c. heavy cream, scalded
        whipped cream, for garnish
        julienne of candied ginger, for garnish

julienne of carrot, for garnish

Directions:

1. In large saucepan, over medium heat, cook carrots with butter, sugar, and rice until carrots begin to soften. Add broth and bring to a simmer.
2. When rice is tender, add ginger; simmer 5 minutes.
3. Purée solids in a blender.
4. Whisk hot cream into soup; bring back to a simmer.
5. Keep soup hot in a double boiler, covered with a lid.
6. Garnish with whipped cream, ginger, and carrot.

Strawberry Tropical Soup

This is a heavenly soup with a taste of lime, and is very satisfying served as a light lunch.

Ingredients:

3 c. strawberries
1 c. frozen cherries, thawed
1 sm. can crushed pineapple, drained
4 c. frozen strawberry juice, diluted
2 Tbs. honey
½ c. fresh lime juice
½ c. light cream
2 Tbs. cornstarch
2 Tbs. cold water
½ c. sour cream

Directions:

1. In small cup, mix cornstarch in water.
2. In large saucepan, over low heat, combine strawberry juice, honey, and lime juice; simmer until mixture thickens. Remove from heat.
3. Stir occasionally as mixture cools.
4. Add strawberries and cream; blend until smooth.
5. Strain through a strainer.
6. Mix in cherries and pineapple.
7. Add a dollop of sour cream to each dish before serving.

Cold Strawberry Soup

This is a nice soup to serve before a meal of roasted poultry or pork.

Ingredients:

    2 pt. strawberries, fresh or frozen (14 oz.)
    ½ c. sugar
    2 c. heavy cream
    2 c. milk
    8 strawberries, for garnish

Directions:

1. Hull fresh berries or thaw frozen berries; rinse under cold water.
2. In a food processor, purée berries with sugar.
3. Let sit overnight.
4. In medium bowl, whip cream until thickened, but not stiff.
5. Fold together cream, milk, and berry mixture.
6. Slice remaining berries from tip almost to the stem.
7. Serve in chilled soup bowls.
8. Hang strawberries on the side.

Rhubarb Mascarpone Soup

Ginger and vanilla add fragrance and flavor to this rhubarb soup.

Ingredients:

    1 rhubarb stalk, cut into angled 1-inch pieces
    2 Tbs. sugar
    1 pc. ginger stem, sliced
    1 vanilla pod, split
    1 c. water
    1 Tbs. mascarpone cheese

Directions:

1. In frying pan, add rhubarb and all other ingredients except the mascarpone.
2. Simmer for 3 to 4 minutes, until rhubarb is tender.
3. Remove rhubarb and put in a small serving dish.
4. Simmer remaining juice for 1 minute.
5. Add to the rhubarb.
6. Top with a spoonful of mascarpone cheese; serve.

Tomato Soup with Salmon

This is simply a change of pace to spark up a canned soup. It is easy to make if you are short on time and want to make something special. It is delicious served with a salad and your favorite bread or rolls, as well as the crackers.

Ingredients:

smoked salmon, broken into small chunks
oyster crackers
any tomato soup

Directions:

1. In large saucepan, heat soup.
2. Stir in salmon chunks.
3. Serve hot with oyster crackers.

Did You Know? . . . .

Did you know that Cupid, another symbol of Valentine's Day, became associated with it because he was the son of Venus, the Roman god of love and beauty? Cupid often appears on Valentine cards holding a bow and arrows because he is believed to use magical arrows to inspire feelings of love.

Cranberry Soup

This soup is great for a brunch or luncheon, served with cold chicken or turkey sandwiches.

Ingredients:

2 c. fresh or frozen cranberries
2 c. apple juice
1 c. fresh or frozen unsweetened raspberries, thawed
1 c. sugar
1 Tbs. lemon juice
¼ tsp. ground cinnamon
2 c. half and half cream, divided
1 Tbs. cornstarch
whipping cream (optional)
raspberries, for garnish (optional)

Directions:

1. In 3-quart saucepan, bring cranberries and apple juice to a boil.
2. Reduce heat and simmer, uncovered, for 10 minutes.
3. Press mixture through a sieve; discard skins and seeds, and return liquid to the pan; bring to boil.
4. Add sugar, lemon juice, and cinnamon; remove from heat; and cool 4 minutes.
5. Stir 1 cup of fruit mixture into 1½ cups half and half.
6. Return all to saucepan; bring to a gentle boil.
7. Mix cornstarch with remaining half and half; stir into soup.
8. Cook and stir for 2 minutes.
9. Serve hot or chilled.
10. Garnish with whipped cream and raspberries, if desired.

Valentine Delights Cookbook
A Collection of Valentine Recipes
Cookbook Delights Holiday Series - Book 2

Wines and Spirits

Table of Contents

Page

About Cooking with Alcohol

Some recipes in this cookbook contain, among other ingredients, liquors. It is for the purpose of obtaining desired flavor and achieving culinary appreciation and not to be abused in any way. In cooking and baking, alcohol evaporates and only the flavor may be enjoyed. When mixed in cold, however, such as in desserts, caution must be exercised. These recipes are intended for people who may consume small amounts of alcohol in a responsible and safe manner.

I live in Washington State and we are proud of our wine production. Washington State is rapidly gaining prestige as a premier wine producer. Do enjoy the art of wine tasting and enjoy the completeness and uniqueness of each wine. It is an art to enjoy and savor in moderation.

If consumption of even small amounts of alcoholic ingredients presents a problem, in whatever form, please substitute coffee flavor syrups, found in coffee sections of supermarkets. For example, instead of Southern Comfort liqueur, substitute with Irish Cream or Amaretto Syrup.

Karen Jean Matsko Hood

Did You Know? . . . .

Did you know that California produces 60 percent of American roses, but the vast number sold on Valentine's Day in the United States are imported, mostly from South America? Approximately 110 million roses, the majority red, will be sold and delivered within a three-day time period.

Did you know that in the United States, 64 percent of men do not make plans in advance for a romantic Valentine's Day with their sweethearts?

Aphrodite's Love Potion

This is a sweet and brightly colored drink. Serve it to your sweetie on Valentine's Day.

Ingredients:

    4   ice cubes
    1½ oz. fine brandy
    5   oz. pineapple juice
    1   maraschino cherry
    1   orange, thinly sliced

Directions:

1. In a tall glass, combine ice cubes, brandy, and pineapple juice; stir.
2. Garnish with cherry and orange slice.

Comfortable Love

This is another drink with the spirit of Valentine's Day in mind.

Ingredients:

    ½   oz. sloe gin
    ½   oz. southern comfort
    ½   oz. vodka
    1½ oz. orange juice
        crushed ice

Directions:

1. In shaker jar, combine all ingredients with crushed ice; shake well.
2. Pour into a glass.

Cherry Sorbet

This is a nice sorbet that is very refreshing to serve your sweetie on Valentine's Day or any other special occasion.

Ingredients:

1 c. water
½ c. sweet white wine
⅓ c. sugar
1½ lb. cherries, pitted
¼ c. lemon juice
2 Tbs. maraschino cherries, diced

Directions:

1. In a nonreactive saucepan, combine water, sugar, and cherries; bring to a boil.
2. Simmer for 5 minutes.
3. Remove from heat and let cool.
4. In blender or food processor, purée the mixture.
5. Strain through fine sieve to remove the skins.
6. In large bowl, combine this mixture with the rest of the ingredients.
7. Either use an ice cream maker and follow the manufacturer's instructions, or place in a tall canister and put in the freezer.
8. Freeze for 1½ hours.
9. Remove from freezer; stir and beat briefly with a whisk.
10. Return to freezer and repeat the beating process after another 50 minutes.
11. You may have to repeat this process three or four times.
12. The more you beat your sorbet, the more air is being incorporated and hence the lighter the finished product.

13. Keep in the freezer above your refrigerator rather than a deep freeze; otherwise you will get a finished product that is hard.
14. If you only have a deep freeze, place sorbet in refrigerator for 1 to 2 hours before serving.
15. This will keep for 3 or 4 days.

Strawberries with Champagne

What nicer way to relax with your loved one and spoil them than serving champagne and chocolate strawberries on Valentine's Day!

Ingredients:

    1 jar chocolate hazelnut spread
      fresh strawberries, stems intact
      heavy cream
      champagne, chilled

Directions:

1. Buy large, fresh strawberries that have their stems intact.
2. A few hours before using, wash, pat dry, and refrigerate the strawberries. Cold strawberries will cause the chocolate to harden and there will be less dripping.
3. Place 1 cup of the chocolate hazelnut spread in a double boiler or fondue pot.
4. Add 1 to 2 tablespoons of heavy cream.
5. Heat over low heat.
6. Add more heavy cream as needed until the consistency of heavy cream.
7. Have your strawberries ready for dipping and serve them to your Valentine.

Cupid's Cosmopolitan

This red citrus-flavored cocktail makes a colorful drink.

Ingredients:

  1 oz. cranberry juice
  2 oz. Grand Marnier
  3 oz. vodka
  1 oz. lime juice
    crushed ice
    lime slices, for garnish
    cranberry branch, for garnish

Directions:

  1. In shaker jar, combine all ingredients with crushed ice; shake well.
  2. Pour into a chilled double cocktail glass.
  3. Garnish with lime slice and a branch of cranberries.

Man of the Moment

This drink is made with scotch, hence the name.

Ingredients:

  1½ oz. scotch
  1   oz. Grand Marnier
  1   oz. lemon juice
  1   tsp. grenadine

Directions:

  1. In shaker jar, half filled with ice cubes, combine ingredients; shake well.
  2. Strain into a cocktail glass.

Valentine's Day Cocktails

If you have never eaten passion fruit or tried its nectar, you are in for a treat with this drink. It is absolutely delicious.

Ingredients:

    1 c. passion fruit blend nectar, chilled
    ½ tsp. angostura bitters
    1 c. champagne or other sparkling white wine, chilled
    4 fresh raspberries or small strawberries
    1 orange slice, cut in half

Directions:

    1. Divide nectar and bitters between two chilled
       champagne flutes.
    2. Add champagne.
    3. Drop 2 berries into each drink.
    4. Garnish with orange slice.

Strawberry Champagne Punch

The strawberries and ginger ale liven up the champagne and make a great tasting punch.

Ingredients:

    1 bottle champagne, chilled
    2 qt. ginger ale, chilled
    12 oz. frozen strawberries

Directions:

    1. In large punch bowl, combine champagne, ginger
       ale, and strawberries.
    2. Stir gently and serve.

Piña Colada

This is a twist on the classic version of a piña colada.

Ingredients:

- 1 lemon
- 1 Tbs. sugar
- 4 slices canned pineapple
- 1 bottle white wine
- 2 c. lemon lime flavored carbonated beverage

Directions:

1. Wash lemon well and cut into fine slices.
2. Put in a gallon jar with sugar.
3. Mince pineapple and put in jar.
4. Pour in wine and soda.
5. Mix with a spoon and refrigerate for 2 hours.

Valentine's Sangria

Sangria is a blend of fruits and wine and is very potent as well as flavorful.

Ingredients:

- 2 bottles red wine
- 4 c. rum, divided
- 4 c. orange juice, divided
- 1 c. sugar
- 1 can pineapple chunks in juice (20 oz.)
- 1 jar maraschino cherries (10 oz.)

Directions:

1. In large pitcher, mix red wine, 2 cups rum, 2 cups orange juice, and sugar.

2. Refrigerate at least 8 hours.
3. In large bowl, mix strawberries, pineapple chunks, and maraschino cherries.
4. Cover with remaining rum and orange juice.
5. Refrigerate at least 8 hours.
6. Drain the fruit, reserving amount of liquid desired.
7. Mix the fruit into the pitcher with the sangria to serve.

Strawberry Margarita Fizz

This is a sweet drink that is very pretty and tasty.

Ingredients:

1½ c. strawberry ice cream, softened
½ c. strawberries, chopped
1   oz. tequila
½ tsp. fresh lime juice
⅓ c. club soda, chilled
  sugar, for coating rims of glasses
  whole strawberries, for garnish
  lime slices, for garnish

Directions:

1. Rub rims of two chilled, stemmed glasses with water and dip in sugar to coat.
2. In blender, combine ice cream, strawberries, tequila, and lime juice.
3. Blend until smooth, but still thick.
4. Pour into glasses.
5. Add club soda.
6. Garnish with whole strawberries and lime slices.

Yields: 2 drinks.

Red Wine Sangria

Sangria is often served in European countries, and it is an enjoyable refreshment.

Ingredients:

1 orange, sliced, for garnish
1 liter club soda, chilled
2 bottles dry red wine, chilled
½ c. orange soda, chilled
1 can lemon lime soda, chilled (12 oz.)
   zest of 1 orange
   ice cubes

Directions:

1. Put the orange zest and orange slices in a pitcher.
2. Add wine and a few ice cubes; stir.
3. Add club soda, lemon lime soda, and orange soda.
4. Serve in wine glasses.

Irish Rose

This is a very refreshing drink. Enjoy!

Ingredients:

1 oz. Tequila Rose strawberry cream liqueur
1 oz. Bailey's Irish cream
1 oz. brown Crème de Cacao

Directions:

1. Pour ingredients into a stainless steel shaker over ice.
2. Shake until completely cold. Strain into a chilled glass.

Valentine's Day Cherry Bomb

Though there are no cherries in this drink, it still has the flavor of them.

Ingredients:

 1 oz. brandy
 ½ oz. triple sec
 1 oz. cream
 1 tsp. grenadine
 4 ice cubes

Directions:

1. In shaker jar, combine brandy, triple sec, cream, grenadine, and ice cubes; shake well.
2. Strain into glass.
3. Serve in a large cup.

Valentine's Day Rum Cream

This is a very sweet and rich drink. Don't forget to refrigerate overnight as it is comparable to eggnog.

Ingredients:

 8 oz. rum
 1 can sweetened condensed milk (14 oz.)
 1 egg
 1 Tbs. vanilla extract

Directions:

1. In blender, combine rum, milk, egg, and vanilla.
2. Blend on medium speed for several minutes.
3. Refrigerate overnight.
4. Serve in tall glasses.

Strawberry Daiquiri

Strawberry daiquiris are delightful and one of my favorites.

Ingredients:

  5 strawberries
  2 oz. light rum
  1 oz. lime juice
  ½ oz. superfine sugar
  1 c. ice

Directions:

1. Place strawberries in blender; blend at high speed until smooth.
2. Add rum, lime juice, and sugar, blending well.
3. Pour into a tall glass and serve with a straw.

Strawberry Martini

This is a unique twist on the classic martini, and it is easy to make right at home for a refreshing drink.

Ingredients:

  2 shots gin
  1 dash dry vermouth
  1 dash strawberry syrup
  1 strawberry

Directions:

1. In large bowl, stir together the gin, vermouth, and strawberry syrup.
2. Strain into chilled cocktail glass.
3. Decorate with a fresh strawberry.

Batida Morango

If you have not tried Cachaca, you will need to try it with strawberries.

Ingredients:

2 oz. Cachaca
½ tsp. sugar
1 c. ice, crushed
5 strawberries, very ripe

Directions:

1. Place all ingredients into a blender; blend well.
2. Pour into a wine glass and serve.

Milky Way

Strawberry and almond flavors combine with pineapple juice to make a very refreshing drink.

Ingredients:

6 parts gin
6 parts amaretto
2 parts strawberry liqueur
3 parts strawberry syrup
   pineapple juice
   slices of apple, lemon, pineapple, for garnish

Directions:

1. Fill a highball glass to the rim with ice cubes.
2. Pour all ingredients except garnish into a shaker.
3. Fill shaker jar with ice cubes; shake until very cold.
4. Strain the drink into the highball glass.
5. Top up with pineapple juice.
6. Garnish with fruit slices and a pineapple leaf.

Midsummer's Night Dream

Cherry brandy adds a nice touch to this strawberry drink.

Ingredients:

    2 oz. vodka
    1 oz. cherry brandy
    1 tsp. strawberry liqueur
    5 fresh strawberries
        sparkling tonic water

Directions:

1. Add ice to a shaker.
2. In blender, add strawberries; purée. Pour into shaker.
3. Add vodka, brandy, and liqueur; shake well.
4. Pour into a highball glass; fill up with tonic water.

Strawberry Coffee Drink

Coffee flavor sets this strawberry drink apart from others. The vanilla schnapps adds a warm taste and fragrance.

Ingredients:

    1 part strawberry cream liqueur
    1 part vanilla schnapps
    1 part coffee liqueur
    1 part cream
    1 splash grenadine syrup

Directions:

1. Pour all ingredients over ice in a shaker; shake well.
2. Strain.
3. Pour into a rocks glass.

Strawberry Hummingbird

This delightful drink blends the flavors of strawberry rum, coffee cream, and bananas. Enjoy!

Ingredients:

½ banana
1 oz. cream
1 oz. rum cream liqueur
1 oz. rum and coffee liqueur
½ oz. strawberry syrup
   crushed ice

Directions:

1. In blender, add banana and cream; blend until smooth.
2. Add liqueurs and strawberry syrup, blending well.
3. To serve, pour over crushed ice in a tall glass.

Banana Berry Shot

This is a simple yet flavorful drink to try.

Ingredients:

1 part Crème de Banana
1 part strawberry schnapps
1 part Crème de Cacao

Directions:

1. Pour each of the three ingredients into a shot glass.
2. Stir.

Strawberry Kiss

This is a pleasing tropical blend with additional flavors of strawberries and peaches.

Ingredients:

1 oz. strawberry liqueur
1 oz. peach schnapps
1 oz. orange juice
1 oz. pineapple juice
1 dash grenadine
1 splash cream
    strawberries, halved
    ice cubes

Directions:

1. Pour alcohol into glass over several ice cubes.
2. Add juices, followed by grenadine and cream.
3. Garnish with strawberry half.

Fruit Surprise

This is a delicious fruit drink that is refreshing and easy to make.

Ingredients:

2 oz. strawberry schnapps
2 oz. orange juice
2 oz. cranberry juice
    club soda

Directions:

1. Pour schnapps, orange juice, and cranberry juice over ice in a highball glass.
2. Top with club soda and serve.

Mexican Strawberry Rose

This makes a festive and colorful drink for entertaining or just a get together with a couple of friends.

Ingredients:

⅔ oz. tequila
⅓ oz. strawberry liqueur
1½ oz. milk
½ oz. grenadine
   lime slices
   strawberry halves

Directions:

1. Place tequila and strawberry liqueur into a shaker; add milk and grenadine.
2. Cover; shake all ingredients together.
3. To serve, strain into ice-filled glass with a slice of lime and strawberry half on toothpick.

Sparkling Strawberry Mimosa

This is a wonderful drink to serve your sweetie on Valentine's Day or any other special time together.

Ingredients:

2 oz. frozen strawberries, sliced
2 oz. orange juice
2 oz. champagne, chilled
   whole fresh strawberries

Directions:

1. In blender, combine berries and juice; blend until smooth.
2. Pour into stemmed glass over ice.
3. Fill with champagne; garnish with strawberries.

Strawberry Fields

This is a smooth, delicious drink. Enjoy!

Ingredients:

    2 shots Cointreau
    1 shot strawberry vodka
    1 shot vodka
    2 shots strawberry liqueur
    1 shot lime juice
      ice
      strawberries

Directions:

1. Shake all ingredients with ice in cocktail shaker.
2. Strain into cocktail glass.
3. Decorate with a strawberry on the glass rim.
4. You can also serve it with ice cubes in a rocks glass.

Spunky Lemonade

This lemonade spiked with orange liqueur and vodka is delicious.

Ingredients:

    1¼ oz. vodka
    ½ oz. orange liqueur
    4   oz. lemonade
    1   Tbs. strawberries, puréed
      crushed ice
      lemon slices

Directions:

1. In blender, add all ingredients and ice; blend until smooth.
2. Pour into a tall glass; garnish with a lemon slice.

Berry Patch

Crème de Cacao and berries and cream make a rich Valentine drink or a special drink any time.

Ingredients:

> ½ oz. strawberry schnapps
> ½ oz. raspberry schnapps
> ½ oz. white Crème de Cacao
>   lemon lime soda
>   half and half cream

Directions:

1. Combine the schnapps and Crème de Cacao in a tall glass.
2. Fill the glass almost to the top with soda.
3. Top with cream and stir gently.

Blushing Peach Cocktail

This peach cocktail has a unique flavor combination and is easy to make. Enjoy!

Ingredients:

> 3 c. raspberry juice, chilled
> 3 c. peach nectar, chilled
>   peach slices, for garnish
>   fresh raspberries, for garnish

Directions:

1. In a large pitcher, combine juices.
2. Pour into glasses over ice.
3. Garnish each glass with a peach slice and raspberry if desired.

Peach Champagne Slush

Champagne is a popular drink and this version is a delicious one that your special person will appreciate.

Ingredients:

 3½ c. fresh peaches, peeled, sliced
 ⅓ c. sugar
 ½ c. peach schnapps
 1 c. pink champagne
   lime slices, cut in half, for garnish

Directions:

 1. In blender container, add peaches, sugar, and peach schnapps; blend until smooth.
 2. Add champagne and stir well.
 3. Pour in shallow baking dish; freeze at least 3 hours.
 4. Place in blender and pulse to slush consistency.
 5. Pour into chilled champagne glasses.
 6. Place a half lime slice on rim of each glass.

Peach Cranberry Juice

Vodka and peach schnapps are topped off with a splash of cranberry juice in this beverage, making a great hit for a party!

Ingredients:

 1.5 fl. oz. jigger peach schnapps
 1.5 fl. oz. jigger vodka
 2 fl. oz. cranberry juice

Directions:

 1. In a small, chilled glass, stir together the peach schnapps and vodka.
 2. Add ice cubes; top with a splash of cranberry juice.
 3. Stir and serve immediately.

Frozen Peach Daiquiris

After you taste one of these, you will know why you decided to put one together!

Ingredients for peach ice cubes:

- 4   fresh peaches, peeled, sliced
- 1   Tbs. lemon juice

Ingredients for drink:

2½ oz. dark rum
¼ c. lime juice, freshly squeezed
¼ c. sugar
¾ c. crushed ice
    peach and lime slices, for garnish

Directions for peach ice cubes to make ahead:

1. In blender, combine peaches and lemon juice; cover and purée until smooth.
2. Pour into ice cube trays; freeze.

Directions for drink:

1. In blender, combine rum, lime juice, sugar, crushed ice, and peach ice cubes; cover and blend until smooth.
2. Pour into chilled, stemmed glasses.
3. Garnish with peach and lime slices on a wooden pick.
4. Serve immediately.
5. Note: For nonalcoholic version, substitute pineapple juice for rum and decrease sugar to 2 tablespoons.

Yields: 3 to 4 servings.

Festival Information

Valentine's Day Pro/Am Chocolate Festival
Logan Chamber Of Commerce
160 N. Main Street
Logan, UT 84321-4541
Phone: 1-435-752-2161

City of Love Festival
Glasgow, Scotland
Mid February each year

U.S. and Metric Measurement Charts

Here are some measurement equivalents to help you with exchanges. There was a time when many people thought the entire world would convert to the metric scale. While most of the world has, America still has not. Metric conversions in cooking are vitally important to preparing a tasty recipe. Here are simple conversion tables that should come in handy.

U.S. Measurement Equivalents

a few grains/pinch/dash (dry) = less than ⅛ teaspoon
a dash (liquid) = a few drops
3 teaspoons = 1 tablespoon
½ tablespoon = 1½ teaspoons
1 tablespoon = 3 teaspoons
2 tablespoons = 1 fluid ounce
4 tablespoons = ¼ cup
5⅓ tablespoons = ⅓ cup
8 tablespoons = ½ cup
8 tablespoons = 4 fluid ounces
10⅔ tablespoons = ⅔ cup
12 tablespoons = ¾ cup
16 tablespoons = 1 cup
16 tablespoons = 8 fluid ounces
⅛ cup = 2 tablespoons
¼ cup = 4 tablespoons
¼ cup = 2 fluid ounces
⅓ cup = 5 tablespoons plus 1 teaspoon
½ cup = 8 tablespoons
1 cup = 16 tablespoons
1 cup = 8 fluid ounces
1 cup = ½ pint
2 cups = 1 pint
2 pints = 1 quart
4 quarts (liquid) = 1 gallon
8 quarts (dry) = 1 peck
4 pecks (dry) = 1 bushel
1 kilogram = approximately 2 pounds
1 liter = approximately 4 cups or 1 quart

Approximate Metric Equivalents by Volume

U.S.	Metric
¼ cup	60 milliliters
½ cup	120 milliliters
1 cup	230 milliliters
1¼ cups	300 milliliters
1½ cups	360 milliliters
2 cups	460 milliliters
2½ cups	600 milliliters
3 cups	700 milliliters
4 cups (1 quart)	.95 liter
1.06 quarts	1 liter
4 quarts (1 gallon)	3.8 liters

Approximate Metric Equivalents by Weight

U.S.	Metric
¼ ounce	7 grams
½ ounce	14 grams
1 ounce	28 grams
1¼ ounces	35 grams
1½ ounces	40 grams
2½ ounces	70 grams
4 ounces	112 grams
5 ounces	140 grams
8 ounces	228 grams
10 ounces	280 grams
15 ounces	425 grams
16 ounces (1 pound)	454 grams

Glossary

Aerate: A synonym for sift; to pass ingredients through a fine-mesh device to break up large pieces and incorporate air into ingredients to make them lighter.

Al dente: "To the tooth," in Italian. The pasta is cooked just enough to maintain a firm, chewy texture.

Baste: To brush or spoon liquid fat or juices over meat during roasting to add flavor and prevent drying out.

Bias-slice: To slice a food crosswise at a 45-degree angle.

Bind: To thicken a sauce or hot liquid by stirring in ingredients such as eggs, flour, butter, or cream until it holds together.

Blackened: Popular Cajun-style cooking method. Seasoned foods are cooked over high heat in a super-heated heavy skillet until charred.

Blanch: To scald, as in vegetables being prepared for freezing; as in almonds so as to remove skins.

Blend: To mix or fold two or more ingredients together to obtain equal distribution throughout the mixture.

Braise: To brown meat in oil or other fat, and then cook slowly in liquid. The effect of braising is to tenderize the meat.

Bread: To coat food with crumbs (usually with soft or dry bread crumbs), sometimes seasoned.

Brown: To quickly sauté, broil, or grill either at the beginning or at the end of meal preparation, often to enhance flavor, texture, or eye appeal.

Brush: To use a pastry brush to coat a food such as meat or pastry with melted butter, glaze, or other liquid.

Butterfly: To cut open a food such as pork chops down the center without cutting all the way through, and then spread apart.

Caramelization: Browning sugar over a flame, with or without the addition of some water to aid the process. The temperature range in which sugar caramelizes is approximately 320 to 360 degrees F.

Clarify: To remove impurities from butter or stock by heating the liquid, then straining or skimming it.

Coddle: A cooking method in which foods (such as eggs) are put in separate containers and placed in a pan of simmering water for slow, gentle cooking.

Confit: To slowly cook pieces of meat in their own gently rendered fat.

Core: To remove the inedible center of fruits such as pineapples.

Cream: To beat vegetable shortening, butter, or margarine, with or without sugar, until light and fluffy. This process traps in air bubbles, later used to create height in cookies and cakes.

Crimp: To create a decorative edge on a pie crust. On a double pie crust, this also seals the edges together.

Curd: A custard-like pie or tart filling flavored with juice and zest of citrus fruit, usually lemon, although lime and orange may also be used.

Curdle: To cause semisolid pieces of coagulated protein to develop in food, usually as a result of the addition of an acid substance or the overheating of milk or egg-based sauces.

Custard: A mixture of beaten egg, milk, and possibly other ingredients such as sweet or savory flavorings, which are cooked with gentle heat, often in a water bath or double boiler. As pie filling, the custard is frequently cooked and chilled before being layered into a baked crust.

Deglaze: To add liquid to a pan in which foods have been fried or roasted, in order to dissolve the caramelized juices stuck to the bottom of the pan.

Dot: To sprinkle food with small bits of an ingredient such as butter to allow for even melting.

Dredge: To sprinkle lightly and evenly with sugar or flour. A dredger has holes pierced on the lid to sprinkle evenly.

Drippings: The liquids left in the bottom of a roasting or frying pan after meat is cooked. Drippings are generally used for gravies and sauces.

Drizzle: To pour a liquid such as a sweet glaze or melted butter in a slow, light trickle over food.

Dust: To sprinkle food lightly with spices, sugar, or flour for a light coating.

Egg Wash: A mixture of beaten eggs (yolks, whites, or whole eggs) and either milk or water. Used to coat cookies and other baked goods to give them a shine when baked.

Emulsion: A mixture of liquids, one being a fat or oil and the other being water based so that tiny globules of one are suspended in the other. This may involve the use of stabilizers, such as egg or custard. Emulsions may be temporary or permanent.

Entrée: A French term that originally referred to the first course of a meal, served after the soup and before the meat courses. In the United States, it refers to the main dish of a meal.

Fillet: To remove the bones from meat or fish for cooking.

Filter: To remove lumps, excess liquid, or impurities by passing through paper or cheesecloth.

Firm-Ball Stage: In candy making, the point at which boiling syrup dropped in cold water forms a ball that is compact yet gives slightly to the touch.

Flambé: To ignite a sauce or other liquid so that it flames.

Flan: An open pie filled with sweet or savory ingredients; also, a Spanish dessert of baked custard covered with caramel.

Flute: To create a decorative scalloped or undulating edge on a pie crust or other pastry.

Fricassee: Usually a stew in which the meat is cut up, lightly cooked in butter, and then simmered in liquid until done.

Frizzle: To cook thin slices of meat in hot oil until crisp and slightly curly.

Ganache: A rich chocolate filling or coating made with chocolate, vegetable shortening, and possibly heavy cream. It can coat cakes or cookies and be used as a filling for truffles.

Glaze: A liquid that gives an item a shiny surface. Examples are fruit jams that have been heated or chocolate thinned with melted vegetable shortening. Also, to cover a food with such a liquid.

Gratin: To bind together or combine food with a liquid such as cream, milk, béchamel sauce, or tomato sauce in a shallow dish. The mixture is then baked until cooked and set.

Hard-Ball Stage: In candy making, the point at which syrup has cooked long enough to form a solid ball in cold water.

Hull (also husk): To remove the leafy parts of soft fruits, such as strawberries or blackberries.

Infusion: To extract flavors by soaking them in liquid heated in a covered pan. The term also refers to the liquid resulting from this process.

Jerk or Jamaican Jerk Seasoning: A dry mixture of various spices such as chilies, thyme, garlic, onions, and cinnamon or cloves used to season meats such as chicken or pork.

Julienne: To cut into long, thin strips.

Jus: The natural juices released by roasting meats.

Larding: To inset strips of fat into pieces of meat, so that the braised meat stays moist and juicy.

Marble: To gently swirl one food into another.

Marinate: To combine food with aromatic ingredients to add flavor.

Meringue: Egg whites beaten until they are stiff, then sweetened. It can be used as the topping for pies or baked as cookies.

Mull: To slowly heat cider with spices and sugar.

Parboil: To partly cook in a boiling liquid.

Peaks: The mounds made in a mixture. For example, egg white that has been whipped to stiffness. Peaks are "stiff" if they stay upright or "soft" if they curl over.

Pesto: A sauce usually made of fresh basil, garlic, olive oil, pine nuts, and cheese. The ingredients are finely chopped and then mixed, uncooked, with pasta. Generally, the term refers to any uncooked sauce made of finely chopped herbs and nuts.

Pipe: To force a semisoft food through a bag (either a pastry bag or a plastic bag with one corner cut off) to decorate food.

Pressure Cooking: To cook using steam trapped under a locked lid to produce high temperatures and achieve fast cooking time.

Purée: To mash or sieve food into a thick liquid.

Ramekin: A small baking dish used for individual servings of sweet and savory dishes.

Reduce: To cook liquids down so that some of the water evaporates.

Refresh: To pour cold water over freshly cooked vegetables to prevent further cooking and to retain color.

311

Roux: A cooked paste usually made from flour and butter, used to thicken sauces.

Sauté: To cook foods quickly in a small amount of oil in a skillet or sauté pan over direct heat.

Scald: To heat a liquid, usually a dairy product, until it almost boils.

Sear: To seal in a meat's juices by cooking it quickly using very high heat.

Seize: To form a thick, lumpy mass when melted (usually applies to chocolate).

Sift: To remove large lumps from a dry ingredient such as flour or confectioners' sugar by passing it through a fine mesh. This process also incorporates air into the ingredients, making them lighter.

Simmer: To cook food in a liquid at a low enough temperature that small bubbles begin to break the surface.

Steam: To cook over boiling water in a covered pan. This method keeps foods' shape, texture, and nutritional value intact better than methods such as boiling.

Steep: To soak dry ingredients (tea leaves, ground coffee, herbs, spices, etc.) in liquid until the flavor is infused into the liquid.

Stewing: To brown small pieces of meat, poultry, or fish, then simmer them with vegetables or other ingredients in enough liquid to cover them, usually in a closed pot on the stove, in the oven, or with a slow cooker.

Thin: To reduce a mixture's thickness with the addition of more liquid.

Truss: To use string, skewers, or pins to hold together a food to maintain its shape while it cooks (usually applied to meat or poultry).

Unleavened: Baked goods that contain no agents to give them volume, such as baking powder, baking soda, or yeast.

Vinaigrette: A general term referring to any sauce made with vinegar, oil, and seasonings.

Zest: The thin, brightly colored outer part of the rind of citrus fruits. It contains volatile oils, used as a flavoring.

Recipe Index of Valentine Delights

314

Reader Feedback Form

Dear Reader,

We are very interested in what our readers think. Please fill in the form below and return it to:

Whispering Pine Press International, Inc.
c/o Valentine Delights Cookbook
P.O. Box 214, Spokane Valley, WA 99037-0214
Phone: (509) 928-8700 | Fax: (509) 922-9949
Email: sales@whisperingpinepress.com
Publisher Websites: www.WhisperingPinePress.com
www.WhisperingPinePressBookstore.com
Blog: www.WhisperingPinePressBlog.com

Name: _____

Address: _____

City, St., Zip: _____

Phone/Fax: (___) _____ | (___) _____

Email: _____

Comments/Suggestions: _____

_____

_____

_____

_____

A great deal of care and attention has been exercised in the creation of this book. Designing a great cookbook that is original, fun, and easy to use has been a job that required many hours of diligence, creativity, and research. Although we strive to make this book completely error free, errors and discrepancies may not be completely excluded. If you come across any errors or discrepancies, please make a note of them and send them to our publishing office. We are constantly updating our manuscripts, eliminating errors, and improving quality.

Please contact us at the address above.

316

About the Cookbook Delights Series

The *Cookbook Delights Series* includes many different topics and themes. If you have a passion for food and wish to know more information about different foods, then this series of cookbooks will be beneficial to you. Each book features a different type of food, such as avocados, strawberries, huckleberries, salmon, vegetarian, lentils, almonds, cherries, coconuts, lemons, and many, many more.

The *Cookbook Delights Series* not only includes cookbooks about individual foods but also includes several holiday-themed cookbooks. Whatever your favorite holiday may be, chances are we have a cookbook with recipes designed with that holiday in mind. Some examples include *Halloween Delights, Thanksgiving Delights, Christmas Delights, Valentine Delights, Mother's Day Delights, St. Patrick's Day Delights,* and *Easter Delights.*

Each cookbook is designed for easy use and is organized into alphabetical sections. Over 250 recipes are included along with other interesting facts, folklore, and history of the featured food or theme. Each book comes with a beautiful full-color cover, ordering information, and a list of other upcoming books in the series.

Note cards, bookmarks, and a daily journal have been printed and are available to go along with each cookbook. You may view the entire line of cookbooks, journals, cards, posters, puzzles, and bookmarks by visiting our website at www.valentinedelights.com, or you can email us with your questions and your comments to: sales@whisperingpinepress.com.

Please ask your local bookstore to carry these sets of books.

To order, please contact:

Whispering Pine Press International, Inc.
c/o Valentine Delights Cookbook
P.O. Box 214, Spokane Valley, WA 99037-0214
Phone: (509) 928-8700 | Fax: (509) 922-9949
Email: sales@whisperingpinepress.com
Publisher Websites: www.WhisperingPinePress.com
www.WhisperingPinePressBookstore.com
Blog: www.WhisperingPinePressBlog.com
SAN 253-200X

We Invite You to Join the Whispering Pine Press International, Inc., Book Club!

Whispering Pine Press International, Inc.
c/o Valentine Delights Cookbook
P.O. Box 214, Spokane Valley, WA 99037-0214
Phone: (509) 928-8700 | Fax: (509) 922-9949
Email: sales@whisperingpinepress.com
Publisher Websites: www.WhisperingPinePress.com
www.WhisperingPinePressBookstore.com
Blog: www.WhisperingPinePressBlog.com

Buy 11 books and get the next one free, based on the average price of the first eleven purchased.

How the club works:

Simply use the order form below and order books from our catalog. You can buy just one at a time or all eleven at once. After the first eleven books are purchased, the next one is free. Please add shipping and handling as listed on this form. There are no purchase requirements at any time during your membership. Free book credit is based on the average price of the first eleven books purchased.

Join today! Pick your books and mail in the form today!

Yes! I want to join the Whispering Pine Press International, Inc., Book Club! Enroll me and send the books indicated below.

Title	Price
1.	
2.	
3.	
4.	
5.	
6.	
7.	
8.	
9.	
10.	
11.	

Free Book Title: _____

Free Book Price: _____ Avg. Price: _____ Total Price: _____

Credit for the free book is based on the average price of the first 11 books purchased.

(Circle one) Check | Visa | MasterCard | Discover | American Express

Credit Card #: _____ Expiration Date: _____

Name: _____

Address: _____

City: _____ State: _____ Country: _____

Zip/Postal: _____ Phone: (____) _____

Email: _____

Signature _____

Whispering Pine Press International, Inc. Fundraising Opportunities

Fundraising cookbooks are proven moneymakers and great keepsake providers for your group. Whispering Pine Press International, Inc., offers a very special personalized cookbook fundraising program that encourages success to organizations all across the USA.

Our prices are competitive and fair. Currently, we offer a special of 100 books with many free features and excellent customer service. Any purchase you make is guaranteed first-rate.

Flexibility is not a problem. If you have special needs, we guarantee our cooperation in meeting each of them. Our goal is to create a cookbook that goes beyond your expectations. We have the confidence and a record that promises continual success.

Another great fundraising program is the *Cookbook Delights Series* Program. With cookbook orders of 50 copies or more, your organization receives a huge discount, making for a prompt and lucrative solution.

We also specialize in assisting group fundraising – Christian, community, nonprofit, and academic among them. If you are struggling for a new idea, something that will enhance your success and broaden your appeal, Whispering Pine Press International, Inc., can help.

For more information, write, phone, or fax to:

Whispering Pine Press International, Inc.
P.O. Box 214
Spokane Valley, WA 99037-0214
Phone: (509) 928-8700 | Fax: (509) 922-9949
Email: sales@whisperingpinepress.com
Publisher Websites: www.WhisperingPinePress.com
www.WhisperingPinePressBookstore.com
Blog: www.WhisperingPinePressBlog.com
Book Website: www.ValentineDelights.com
SAN 253-200X

Personalized and/or Translated Order Form for Any Book by Whispering Pine Press International, Inc.

Dear Readers:

If you or your organization wishes to have this book or any other of our books personalized, we will gladly accommodate your needs. For instance, if you would like to change the names of the characters in a book to the names of the children in your family or Sunday school class, we would be happy to work with you on such a project. We can add more information of your choosing and customize this book especially for your family, group, or organization.

We are also offering an option of translating your book into another language. Please fill out the form below telling us exactly how you would like us to personalize your book.

Please send your request to:

Whispering Pine Press International, Inc.
c/o Valentine Delights Cookbook
P.O. Box 214, Spokane Valley, WA 99037-0214
Phone: (509) 928-8700 | Fax: (509) 922-9949
Email: sales@whisperingpinepress.com
Publisher Websites: www.WhisperingPinePress.com
www.WhisperingPinePressBookstore.com
Blog: www.WhisperingPinePressBlog.com

Person/Organization placing request: _____

_____ Date: _____

Phone: (____) _____ Fax: (____) _____

Address: _____

City: _____ State: _____ Zip: _____

Language of the book: _____

Please explain your request in detail: _____

_____

_____

_____

_____

Valentine Delights Cookbook
A Collection of Valentine Recipes
How to Order

Get your additional copies of this book by returning an order form and your check, money order, or credit card information to:

Whispering Pine Press International, Inc.
c/o Valentine Delights Cookbook
P.O. Box 214, Spokane Valley, WA 99037-0214
Phone: (509) 928-8700 | Fax: (509) 922-9949
Email: sales@whisperingpinepress.com
Publisher Websites: www.WhisperingPinePress.com
www.WhisperingPinePressBookstore.com
Blog: www.WhisperingPinePressBlog.com

Customer Name: _____

Address: _____

City, St., Zip: _____

Phone/Fax: _____

Email: _____

- -

Please send me _____ copies of _____

_____ at $_____

per copy and $4.95 for shipping and handling per book, plus $2.95 each for additional books. Enclosed is my check, money order, or charge my account for $_____.

☐ Check   ☐ Money Order   ☐ Credit Card

(*Circle One*) MasterCard | Discover | Visa | American Express
☐☐☐☐ ☐☐☐☐ ☐☐☐☐ ☐☐☐☐

Expiration Date: _____

_____
Signature

_____
Print Name

Whispering Pine Press International, Inc. Order Form

Gift-wrapping, Autographing, and Inscription
We are proud to offer personal autographing by the author. For a limited time this service is absolutely free!
Gift-wrapping is also available for $4.95 per item.

1. Sold To
Name: _____
Street/Route: _____
_____
City: _____
State: _____ Zip: _____
Country: _____
Gift message: _____
_____
Email address: _____
Daytime Phone: (_ _ _) _ _ _-_ _ _ _
*Necessary for verifying orders
Home Phone: (_ _ _) _ _ _-_ _ _ _
Fax: (_ _ _) _ _ _-_ _ _ _

2. Ship To
☐ Is this a new or corrected address?

☐ Alternative Shipping Address

☐ Mailing Address
Name: _____
Address: _____
_____
City: _____
State: _____ Zip: _____
Country: _____
Email address: _____

3. Items Ordered

ISBN # /Item #	Size	Color	Qty.	Title or Description	Price	Total

4. Method Of Payment
International, Inc. (No Cash or COD's)

☐ Visa ☐ MasterCard ☐ Discover ☐ American Express ☐ Check/Money Order
Please make it payable to Whispering Pine Press International, Inc. (No Cash or COD's)

Account Number   Expiration Date
_____ /_____
Month Year

☐☐☐☐ ☐☐☐☐ ☐☐☐☐

Signature_____
Cardholder's signature

Printed Name_____
Please print name of cardholder
Address of Cardholder_____

Subtotal	
Gift wrap $4.95 Each	
For delivery in WA add 8.7% sales tax.	
Shipping See chart at left	
6. Total	

5. Shipping & Handling

Continental US
US Postal Ground: For books please add $4.95 for the first book and $2.95 each for additional books.
All non-book items, add 15% of the Subtotal.
Please allow 1-4 weeks for delivery.
US Postal Air: Please add $15.00 shipping and handling.
Please allow 1-3 days for delivery.
Alaska, Hawaii, and the US Territories By Ship:
Please add 10% shipping and handling (minimum charge $15.00).

Please
By Air: Please add 12% shipping and handling (minimum charge $15.00).
Please allow 2–6 weeks for delivery.
International By Ship: Please add 10% shipping and handling (minimum charge $15.00).
Please allow 6-12 weeks for delivery.
By Air: Please add 12% shipping and handling (minimum charge $15.00).
Please allow 2-6 weeks for delivery.
FedEx Shipments: Add $5.00 to the above airmail charges for overnight delivery.

Whispering Pine Press International, Inc.
P.O. Box 214
Spokane Valley, WA 99037-0214 USA
Phone: (509) 928-8700 • Fax: (509) 922-9949
Email: sales@whisperingpinepress.com
Website: www.whisperingpinepress.com

Shop Online:
www.whisperingpinepress.com
Fax orders to: (509) 922-9949

About the Author and Cook

Karen Jean Matsko Hood has always enjoyed cooking, baking, and experimenting with recipes. At this time Hood is working to complete a series of cookbooks that blends her skills and experience in cooking and entertaining. Hood entertains large groups of people and especially enjoys designing creative menus with holiday, international, ethnic, and regional themes.

Hood is publishing a cookbook series entitled the *Cookbook Delights Series*, in which each cookbook emphasizes a different food ingredient or theme. The first cookbook in the series is *Apple Delights Cookbook.* Hood is working to complete another series of cookbooks titled *Hood and Matsko Family Cookbooks*, which includes many recipes handed down from her family heritage and others that have emerged from more current family traditions. She has been invited to speak on talk radio shows on various topics, and favorite recipes from her cookbooks have been prepared on local television programs.

Hood was born and raised in Great Falls, Montana. As an undergraduate, she attended the College of St. Benedict in St. Joseph, Minnesota, and St. John's University in Collegeville, Minnesota. She attended the University of Great Falls in Great Falls, Montana. Hood received a B.S. Degree in Natural Science from the College of St. Benedict and minored in both Psychology and Secondary Education. Upon her graduation, Hood and her husband taught science and math on the island of St. Croix in the U.S. Virgin Islands. Hood has completed postgraduate classes at the University of Iowa in Iowa City, Iowa. In May 2001, she completed her Master's Degree in Pastoral Ministry at Gonzaga University in Spokane, Washington. She has taken postgraduate classes at Lewis and Clark College on the North Idaho college campus in Coeur d'Alene, Idaho, Taylor University in Fort Wayne, Indiana, Spokane Falls Community College, Spokane Community College, Washington State University, University of Washington, and Eastern Washington University. Hood is working on research projects to complete her Ph.D. in Leadership Studies at Gonzaga University in Spokane, Washington.

Hood resides in Greenacres, Washington, along with her husband, sixteen children, and foster children. Her interests include writing, research, and teaching. She previously has volunteered as a court advocate in the Spokane juvenile court system for abused and neglected children. Hood is a literary advocate for youth and adults. Her hobbies include cooking, baking, collecting, photography, indoor and outdoor gardening, farming, and the cultivation of unusual flowering plants and orchids. She enjoys raising several specialty breeds of animals including Babydoll Southdown, Friesen, and Icelandic sheep, Icelandic horses, bichons frisés, cockapoos, Icelandic sheepdogs, a Newfoundland, a Rottweiler, a variety of Nubian and fainting goats, and a few rescue cats. Hood also enjoys bird-watching and finds all aspects of nature precious.

She demonstrates a passionate appreciation of the environment and a respect for all life. She also invites you to visit her websites:

www.KarenJeanMatskoHood.com www.
KarenJeanMatskoHoodBookstore.com
www.KarenJeanMatskoHoodBlog.com
www.KarensKidsBooks.com
www.KarensTeenBooks.com

www.HoodFamilyBlog.com
www.HoodFamily.com

Author's Social Media
Please Follow the Author on **Twitter**: @KarenJeanHood
Friend her on **Facebook**: Karen Jean Matsko Hood Author Fan Page
Google Plus Profile: Karen Jean Matsko Hood
Pinterest.com/KarenJMHood

www.ingramcontent.com/pod-product-compliance
Lightning Source LLC
Chambersburg PA
CBHW031235090426

42742CB00007B/211